CHRIS-CRAFT

Jack Savage

MBI Publishing Company

First published in 2000 by MBI Publishing Company,
729 Prospect Avenue, PO Box 1, Osceola, WI
54020-0001 USA

MBI Publishing Company books are also available at
discounts in bulk quantity for industrial or sales-promotional
use. For details write to Special Sales Manager at
Motorbooks International Wholesalers & Distributors, 729
Prospect Avenue, Osceola, WI 54020-0001 USA.

Library of Congress Cataloging-in-Publication Data Available
ISBN: 0-7603-0606-0

On the front cover: Chris-Craft ruled the lakes in 1955
thanks in part to Runabouts like this Capri. Fitted with an
optional 200 horsepower engine, the 21-foot Capri's
could hit amost 50 miles per hour. *Classic Boating*

On the frontis: The tell-tale bleached mahogany kingplank
of a classic postwar Chris-Craft. *Classic Boating*

On the title pages: The popular Riviera was introduced
in 1949, successor to the 20-foot Custom Runabout.
Featuring a more rounded bow with a two-piece
cutwater, the Riviera came in 16, 18 and 20-foot lengths.
50/50 is a 1950 model 18-footer. *Robert Bruce Duncan*

On the contents page: The 1946 22-foot *Water Color
Classic Boating*

On the back cover: *Miss DeDe*, a 1949 19-foot Racing
Runabout, in a quiet moment at dusk. *Classic Boating*

Editor: Mike Haenggi
Layout Designer: Rebecca Allen

Printed in China

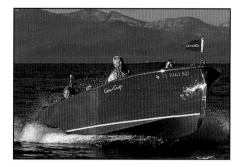

Contents

Acknowledgments

Chris-Craft's long history is rich in lore and detail, and like any writer who attempts to recount some measure of the story of a company and its product, many people have helped me document the history and understand its meaning. At the top of that list are the owners of the classic Chris-Crafts, whose spontaneous enthusiasm launches them into a frenzy of wallet-draining restoration. They save the boats we all love.

Words may inform, but the exquisite photographs bring the old boats to life on the page. I am deeply indebted to Bruce Duncan, photographer extraordinaire, who introduced me to the mahogany world. Equal thanks to Jim and Norm Wangard, publishers of a fine magazine that should grace the desks of all wooden boat enthusiasts, *Classic Boating*.

This book couldn't have been created without the selfless help from Jerry Conrad, John Pemberton, and the rest of the staff at the Mariner's Museum, whose work cataloguing and preserving the Chris-Craft archives benefits all who love the boats.

Thanks also to Tony Mollica, whose enthusiasm and excellent book *Gar Wood Boats* inspired my interest in Chris-Craft; and to former Chris-Craft dealer William Siegenthaler, who helped as well.

And many thanks to Dale Tassell, ardent and informed Chris-Craft historian, as well as Wilson Wright, the seemingly tireless head of the Chris-Craft Antique Boat Club, editor of its newsletter *The Brass Bell*, and moderator of its e-mail list. And many thanks to the many contributors to *The Brass Bell* over the past two decades. Chris-Craft enthusiasts are better off because of their efforts.

Like anyone researching and writing about Chris-Craft, I must acknowledge Jeffrey Rodengen, whose book *The Legend of Chris-Craft* is deservedly considered the bible for Chris lovers. His research in the archives was trailblazing—the rest of us can only follow.

Last but not least, thanks to Zack Miller, Mike Haenggi, Becky Allen, and the others at MBI Publishing whose patience, editorial and design talent turned my modest efforts into a book.

And though all of the above have generously given me their valuable time and lent me their expertise, any mistakes you might find in the ensuing pages are mine alone.
—*Jack Savage*

Above: Instrument cluster on a 1948 25-foot Express Cruiser. Classic Boating

In the foreground, the bleached mahogany glistens on *Harmony*, a 1948 Custom Runabout. *Classic Boating*

Foreword

There she was—a bundle of graying boards on a rusty tubular trailer with two flat tires. But she had classic lines and was touted as a collectable of significant value when restored—and was available, if I'd only pay the storage.

All I knew was she reminded me of boyhood summers in New Hampshire on Lake Winnepesaukee, when the reward for a day's work in the hay field was an aqua-plane ride behind an old woodie. The throaty sound of that big ol' motor came to mind and my emotions overcame me. Before I knew it, a check was written, air was in the tires, and she was hooked to my station wagon. Oh, by the way, did I want the cardboard box of metal parts that was left with her? Sure, what did I know . . . and off I went. I parked her in the driveway, ran a couple of errands, and returned home to find a note on the kitchen counter from two college-age daughters—"Nice Boat, Dad."

Later that day, I looked at her . . . boards to be replaced, compound curves—woodworking way over my head. Under the hatch sat an engine with the head off and cylinders full of water . . . and my mechanical expertise was limited to changing a spark plug. Where did I go from here?

A call to Chris-Craft revealed the existence of a Chris-Craft Antique Boat Club, and a kindly gentleman who told me where to look for a hull number. There it was—stamped in the boat in several places: R 16 148 . . . a number now more permanently imbedded in memory than my social security number. A 1950 16-foot Chris-Craft Riviera, he told me. "Is that good?" I asked. "Rare," he said, adding that if a summer vacation was in store, I might check out a boat show at Weirs Beach on Lake Winnepesaukee. Talk about what goes around . . . and besides there was a pinball machine there that cheated me out of a nickel when I was nine years old. What a chance to get it back and maybe see a boat like mine in the water.

I was to find that I was but a singular part of a growing craze to recoup my misspent youth—some through old cars, old planes, old toys, and, for many, old boats. With the help of many we got the little Riviera in show condition and brought home several

Above: The Riviera, like this 18-foot model *50/50,* remained one of the popular Chris-Crafts among enthusiasts. *Robert Bruce Duncan*

trophies before she was sold in favor of a 19-foot Chris-Craft Racer—a little bigger boat with a little more power. As with the Riv, it was another restoration project whose completion was aided by a growing number of antique boating enthusiasts.

It was A. W. "Mac" MacKerer, known as "Mr. Chris-Craft" after a 40-plus-year career with the company, who suggested in 1973 that it was time to form a club to "encourage the preservation and restoration" of the old Chris-Crafts. Four classes of membership were suggested for (1) original owners, (2) owners of antiques, (3) owners of classics, and (4) those simply interested in antique Chris-Crafts.

In the early days there were but a couple of antique boat shows and the membership of the Chris-Craft Club numbered in the hundreds. But thanks to prominent boatsmen recruited to help the fledgling group—Bruce Barnard, P. V. Carveth, Charles Cross, Gordon Houser, James Irwin, David Kitz, Harvey Moninger, and Jean Vincent (who remains as chairman of the board today)—and many others since, there are now more than 100 antique and classic boat shows and club membership approaching 3000. Web sites abound, on-line discussion groups prompt a hundred or more posts per day, an on-line auction includes dozens of Chris-Craft items, and there's a television program devoted to classic boats.

As for me, that first trip to the Winnepesaukee Antique Boat Show at Weirs Beach led to an introduction to long-time Chris-Craft dealer Jim Irwin, who recruited me to assume the responsibility for administration of the club. It was to be a six-month proposition that is now in its 17th year. I never did get my nickel back from that Weirs Beach pinball machine, but this passion has paid off in so many other meaningful ways.

Indeed, the love of Chris-Crafts and other floating classics is at the heart of America's nostalgia craze and it is only fitting that more be written about them.
—*Wilson Wright*

Wilson Wright, an attorney, is the executive director of the Chris-Craft Antique Boat Club and editor of the club's quarterly newsletter, The Brass Bell. *For membership information, contact the club at 217 South Adams St., Tallahassee, FL 32301-1708.*

The Lake Winnipesaukee Antique Boat Show is one of dozens held across the country where owners and aficionados flock to admire and compare notes on majestic mahogany restorations.

INTRODUCTION

Racing to the Starting Line

There's a certain irony in the fact that mighty Chris-Craft, queen of the pleasure boat industry and virtual inventor of the classic inboard runabout, is now owned by the Outboard Marine Corporation (OMC). The last of the legendary Smith family to oversee Chris-Craft, Harsen Smith said in 1959 that he did not consider outboards a threat. Thirty years later, OMC, one of the world's leading producers of outboard motors, would buy the company out of bankruptcy.

OMC celebrated the 125th anniversary of Chris-Craft in 1999, dating the brand's beginnings back to the first duck boats built by a

Two Racing Runabouts make their owners proud fighting for the lead in a private duel.
In the foreground is a 1953, the other a 1949. *Classic Boating*

Above: Solitude, a 1939 22-footer. *Classic Boating*

Christopher Columbus Smith at the wheel of an early Runabout. Smith was the patriarch of a family dedicated to boatbuilding for years before he and his sons started the company that would become Chris-Craft. *Courtesy Mariners' Museum*

The idea and the timing were perfect, and before the end of the decade, they would make the legitimate claim to be the largest builder of mahogany boats in the world. The early 1930s and the Great Depression forced drastic cutbacks, but with business savvy and a little luck, Chris-Craft would survive. The company would go on to survive numerous other boom-and-bust cycles in the pleasure boating industry.

Chris-Craft's rebound in the late 1930s was interrupted by World War II, but they distinguished themselves as efficient builders of vessels for military use under government contract. After the war, they picked up where they left off, then spawned a new boom in recreational powerboating throughout the 1950s. Runabouts and Utility-style small boats would continue to be popular, and Cruisers would dominate an increasingly diverse Chris-Craft lineup that included Sea Skiff lapstrake hulls, Cavalier division plywood boats, Roamer metal-hulled boats, and even a range of kit boats. The Smith family would sell the company in 1959, ending the first half—and for many enthusiasts the most important half—of the Chris-Craft story in the twentieth century.

Under corporate ownership over the next 20 years, Chris-Craft would convert to the fiberglass construction techniques that took over pleasure boating in the 1960s. There were good years and horrendous years, but Chris-Craft would survive the oil crisis and inflationary 1970s with its reputation for quality intact.

young (13-year-old) Christopher Columbus Smith and his brother in 1874. But Chris-Craft as a brand name, company, and a concept really began in 1922 when Chris Smith and his sons Jay, Bernard, Owen, and Hamilton organized the Chris Smith & Sons Boat Co. with the intent to build standardized boats for everyone.

One of the earliest standardized Runabouts, hull number 15, with Bernard Smith driving owner George Holman's boat. The 26-foot planked hull would have a beam of 6 feet, 6 inches and was powered by a 90-horsepower Curtiss V-8 airplane engine converted for marine use. *Courtesy Mariners' Museum*

Brothers Jay and Bernard Smith helped Gar Wood (center) dominate speedboat racing during the teens. Racing proved a fertile background for the Smiths' later success running Chris-Craft. *Courtesy Mariners' Museum*

Classic Chris-Crafts garner more respect than ever at the numerous boat shows across the country. From left to right, a 1931 Model 300 *Vintage 31*, 1950 16-foot Riviera *Crafty Chris*, 1941 17-foot Runabout *Elizabeth*, and 1948 Runabout *Silver Belle* at the Lake Winnepesaukee Antique and Classic Boat Show.

Murray Industries took over the Chris-Craft boat division during the 1980s, and rode the economic growth of the Reagan years to record revenues. Financial maneuvering led to bankruptcy in 1989, when OMC stepped in to rescue the company. Back under the roof of a company that understands the industry, Chris-Craft survived another recession, thrived again in the 1990s, and is positioned to continue into the twenty-first century as a premier boat builder.

Most Chris-Craft models were never inexpensive—certainly it would have been difficult for the average worker at one of the Chris-Craft plants to afford one—but they were plentiful. Where one-time partner and Chris-Craft rival Gar Wood managed to build fewer than 3,000 boats from 1921 to 1941 (and closed by 1947), it's generally accepted that Chris-Craft built at least 100,000 wooden powerboats from its inception in 1922 through 1972, when the last wooden boat came out of the Holland, Michigan, plant. Approximately 20,000 units were built prior to World War II alone.

And while Chris-Craft is credited with bringing auto industry–style production-line techniques to wooden boat building, their history is made that much more interesting by the use of hull cards. Every boat built was assigned a hull number, and a hull card—much like a job ticket—recorded the details of that particular boat, including dates, materials, colors, and accessories. Those hull cards, for the most part, exist today in the Chris-Craft Collection at the Mariners Museum in Newport News, Virginia.

Consequently, today's owners of classic Chris-Craft Runabouts, Utilities, and Cruisers can usually use the hull number stamped on their boat to research the origin of their specific boat.

Christopher Columbus Smith and the Early Years

Before Chris-Craft, Chris Smith was well known in the boating community as a first-rate boat designer and builder, operating a modest boatyard with his brother on Point du Chene in the small community of Algonac, Michigan. He and his eldest son, Jay, started tinkering with outboards early on, before the turn of the twentieth century, and later Jay would recall that their first gas-powered outboard could make 16 miles per hour—when it ran. In 1910, Smith joined forces with John "Baldy" Ryan, a well-heeled financier who had a home near Algonac, to build raceboats. Before the year was out, the two started the Smith-Ryan Boat Company, which would not only continue to build race-ready single-step hydroplanes for Ryan to compete in, but would also market a line of runabouts offered to the public. At the 1910 National Motor Boat Show in New York, Smith-Ryan displayed a 29-foot, single-step hydroplane called *Queen Reliance*, which they claimed would hit 35 miles per hour.

Ryan introduced Smith to J. Stuart Blackton, powerboat enthusiast and owner of Vitagraph (which would become Warner Bros.). As the story goes, Smith promised Blackton a boat that would top 40 miles per hour or he wouldn't have to pay for it. The result, a single-step hydroplane called *Baby Reliance I*, hit 40-plus with ease, but sank when Blackton and mechanic Jay Smith hit a log.

No matter, the wealthy Blackton quickly ordered up *Baby Reliance II* and *Baby Reliance III*, which would later be renamed *Baby Speed Demon* and capture the prestigious Gold Cup for Blackton in 1914.

By 1913, Ryan was broke, the Smith-Ryan Boat Co. was scuttled, and the Smith clan soldiered on as the C. C. Smith Boat and Engine Company. Then, with World War I draining Blackton's funds, the Smiths were facing hard times.

Chris Smith's next triumph was the *Miss Detroit*, built on spec for a group of Detroit businessmen interested in wresting the Gold Cup from the perennial East Coast contenders. It won going away, but was never paid for—until a fellow named Gar Wood bought it at auction.

Gar Wood, inventor of the hydraulic lift for dump trucks, was the wealthy partner the Smiths needed, and after discussion, Wood became a partner in the C. C. Smith Boat and Engine Company. They combined to dominate speedboat racing for the next six years, winning not only five Gold Cups, but also bringing home the vaunted international Harmsworth Trophy in 1920 with the twin-screw *Miss America I* and *Miss Detroit V*. *Miss America I* would go on to post an international speedboat record of more than 76 miles per hour.

Equally important for the future success of what would become Chris-Craft, Chris Smith's sons, Jay and Bernard,

Though Chris-Craft was successful in large part because of its ability to apply mass production techniques to boatbuilding, individual hull cards created for each boat they built are a testament to the company's attention to detail. Hull cards are now kept as part of the Chris-Craft Collection at the Mariner's Museum in Newport News, Virginia. *Courtesy Mariners' Museum*

Though Chris-Craft's 1930 lineup had expanded, the triple-cockpit 26-foot Runabouts such as *Miss Winnepesaukee* were still the heart of the Smith-built boats. She was sold through Irwin Marine, the oldest continuing Chris-Craft dealer in the country. *Classic Boating*

were well schooled in the boat and engine building trade, acting as drivers and mechanics in the fiercely contested races. In 1921, the Smiths built *Miss America II*, powered by four 500-horsepower Smith-Liberty aircraft engines, which Wood and Jay Smith piloted to a Harmsworth Trophy win over Wood's brother George and Jay's brother Bernard in *Miss America I*. It was a Smith-Wood spectacle of speed and power. *Miss America II* bested 80 miles per hour for a new world record.

But Smith and sons were working on more than race boats during this period. According to research compiled by former Mariner's Museum archivist Tom Crew, the C. C. Smith Boat and Engine Company was using its growing fame as the builders of race boats to reach out to a recreational boating market. In a 1915 ad in *Power Boating* magazine, Chris Smith claims that "most of my business is in building pleasure launches, fast runabouts, express cruisers, and passenger-carrying hydroplanes." In fact, Crew notes, Smith built an 80-foot cruiser named *Hourless* in 1919—a boat larger than any Chris-Craft would ever build.

The August 1921 issue of *Power Boating* carried an ad from Central Marine Service Corporation in Detroit for a "sensational 26-foot express runabout built by Chris Smith as his 1921 standardized boat," selling for $3,950, with a painted finish or with a mahogany hull for $500 more. This early Smith-built runabout followed the norm of the day with the steering kept aft of the engine. Forward cockpit steering controls would soon follow, however.

With six months of that advertisement, Chris Smith and his four sons would unharness themselves from Gar Wood's wealth, take $8,000 in capital, and form Chris Smith & Sons Boat Company.

By the 1950s, Chris-Craft was experimenting with fiberglass and looking to cash in on Detroit-inspired styling. *Jake* is a 1959 19-foot Silver Arrow "designed for the man who wants a modern sports car of the waterways." *Robert Bruce Duncan*

New Rules, New Market

The Smiths' decision to leave Gar Wood and the racing market was well considered. Following Gar Wood's Gold Cup victory in 1921, the American Power Boat Association (APBA) decided that it was time for someone other than the flamboyant industrialist to win in the future. The rules committee not only disallowed aircraft engines, but also the hydroplane hulls that the Smiths had perfected. Instead, competitors were to compete using displacement hulls powered by engines of no more than 625 cubic inches.

While Gar Wood fumed over the obvious attempt to harness his domination of the Gold Cup, the Smiths recognized this as an opportunity. The

Gold Cup would now be essentially a stock boat race, and the displacement hulls would be equally suitable for a family boat. A market was born. They decided to get out from under the racing-dominated influence of Gar Wood and begin again on their own as recreational powerboat builders.

The Wood-Smith partnership may have begun to fall apart when the Smiths took on the task of building not only the race boats that had made Gar Wood world-famous, but boats for Wood's competitors as well—most notably Jesse G. Vincent, chief of engineering for Packard and the designer of Packard's 12-cylinder Liberty aircraft engine used in World War I.

Still, the initial break-away from Gar Wood apparently was amiable, and as Gar Wood historian Anthony Mollica points out in his book *Gar Wood Boats: Classics of a Golden Era*, the Smiths continued to build "Baby Gar" hulls for Wood for a short time.

But ultimately, Gar Wood and the Smiths put their mutual fierce competitive spirits up against each other. Chris Smith & Sons would revolutionize the boatbuilding trade and build Everyman's boat, while Wood targeted the upscale market, stuck with traditional methods, and ultimately ran aground after World War II.

Though the Smiths gave up world-class racing to build pleasure boats for the public, stock racing became popular among Chris-Craft owners. *The Fifth* is a 1941 Racing Runabout with the barrelback stern. *Classic Boating*

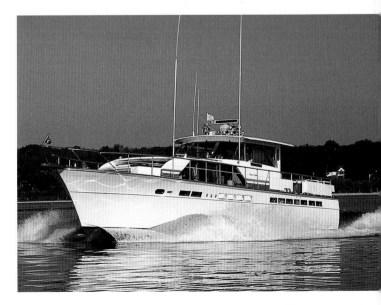

One of Chris-Craft's most enduring cruiser models was the Constellation, first introduced in 1954, including the 57-foot *Pathfinder. Classic Boating*

CHAPTER I

The Standardized Runabout

W hen the Smith family formally created Chris Smith & Sons Boat Company in February 1922, it was hardly a start-up operation. After all, they had been operating as a boat shop for years. However, this incarnation of their business was different—they no longer were helped or handcuffed with a partner from outside the company, and were free to go after what they believed would be a burgeoning recreational powerboat market. They bought 20 acres of land and built a new boat shop after selling their original shop to Gar Wood. It was a fresh beginning. As Motor Boating *magazine would*

Godfather was 1 of 24 boats built by Chris Smith & Sons in 1922, shipped to Gar Wood in October. Owner Wayne Mockfield's 26-foot Runabout was restored by Charlie Gath in New Hampshire, getting a new bottom, sides, and decks. The VI is carved into the original rear seat back. *Classic Boating* Above: *Algonac,* a 1930 28-footer. *Classic Boating*

write eight heady years later, "they banded together, headed by the indomitable Chris, and formally decided to build boats the way that had never been attempted before".

While Chris Smith was and is often given most of the credit for this initiative, and was no doubt a vital source of design expertise and inspiration, it's likely that his sons provided the real energy and determination that drove the business. Chris was then 61, and three of his sons with shares in the new business were Jay, 37; Bernard, 33; and Owen, 27. Jay and Bernard, in particular, were veterans of the business by this time, good engineer/mechanics in their own right, who learned by getting their hands dirty and testing their ideas in competition on the water. By 1927, Jay Smith would be named president and general manager, his brother Bernard installed as vice president and treasurer, and patriarch Chris named chairman of the board.

While Chris Smith & Sons certainly wanted their boats to be known for quality, their goal was not necessarily to build the best boats possible at any cost. Rather—and one of the reasons for their survival and success—they wanted to take a page out of Henry Ford's book and create the best standardized boat that they could build at a reasonable cost and market at a competitive price.

After all, Chris Smith had already had a chance to build the fastest boats in the world through his collaboration with Baldy Ryan, J. Stuart Blackton, and Gar Wood. Now it was time to use the Smith-built reputation created in the racing arena to bring the thrill of motorboating to a wider family market—and make some money in doing so.

In April 1922, they advertised four standard models in *Motor Boat* magazine, including a 24-footer; two 26-foot models, one with a forward-drive double cockpit, the other a rear-drive single cockpit; and a 33-foot "Baby Gar"-style boat. All are referred to as "Chris Smith Craft," no doubt a precursor to what would shortly become Chriscraft.

One of the first Runabouts built by the newly formed Chris Smith & Sons Boat Co., this early 26-footer has two cockpits, one forward and one aft of the midship engine, and came stock with the two wicker chairs. It would have been powered by a converted Curtiss OX-5 aircraft engine. *Courtesy Mariners' Museum*

Chriscraft is Born

Chris' son Hamilton Smith is usually credited with suggesting the name Chriscraft, which appeared initially as one word. (A dubious article in the April 1930 issue of *Motor Boating* magazine credits the name to daughter Catherine.) In any case, for the 1922 Gold Cup races, the first under the new rules limiting engines and requiring displacement hulls, there were numerous Smith-built entries, including a number bearing the name Chriscraft. The winner was the *Packard-Chriscraft* built for Packard founder Colonel Jesse Vincent, who beat out Gar Wood, further fueling what would become a fierce rivalry between Wood and the Smiths. According to Tom Crew's research, a third boat, *Chriscraft II*, also ran the 1922 Gold Cup and bore many resemblances to the Smiths' early standardized runabout, including a single cockpit forward of the engine, a large open rear cockpit with wicker chairs, no windshield, and dark seam compound instead of white deck stripes.

The Standardized Boat

Initially, Smith & Sons looked to traditional boat-building techniques to create and market a standardized boat directly to the public. According to the detail-laden notebooks of A. W. "Mac" MacKerer, the specifications for the company's first standardized boat, to be sold for $3,200 plus tax, included a 26-foot length and a 6-foot, 6-inch beam with a draft of 24 inches. It was to be powered by the 90-horsepower, 8-cylinder Curtis OX-5 engine that the Smiths bought in quantity as surplus from World War I, converted to marine use, and renamed Smith-Curtis, and would reach a speed of 30–32 miles per hour. The forward cockpit was meant to seat three, and the aft cockpit would hold five, including the two wicker chairs.

The 26-foot *River Otter* shows off the classic lines of an early Chris-Craft Carvel hull. The 1928 sales brochure assured prospective buyers that " . . . many women and children who drive Chris-Craft have never driven a motor car . . . " *Classic Boating*

The boats were to be built using five different kinds of wood, primarily Philippine mahogany for the bottom planking, decking, instrument board, toe boards, and seat fronts, plus spruce, ash, butternut, and white oak. Total lumber costs were estimated at $143.70, fittings cost $363.80, and labor was figured at $490.00. (The average hourly wage at the boat shop was around $.65) Motor, installation, and overhead costs were added in to the cost of goods.

In comparison, Ford—who created his constant-speed assembly line in 1913—sold the 1922 Model T in four models (including a "runabout") ranging in price from $348 to $645.

The most influential outsider in the Smith family enterprise was no doubt MacKerer, hired in 1922, according to his son Don MacKerer, "to get production out of a plant having trouble meeting the influx of orders for pleasure craft generated by racing triumphs."

Except for two hiatuses (a brief stint with Rochester Marine in 1925-1926, and during the Depression when the management payroll was whittled down to those named Smith), MacKerer would be a critical player in Chris-Craft production and design for more than 40 years until his retirement in 1965, outlasting even the Smith family's involvement in the recreational boating empire.

The first standardized runabouts evolved, no doubt with input from not only each of the Smiths as well as MacKerer, but also designer Nap Lisee, who had worked for the Smiths since 1905. Lisee would continue to work for Chris Smith & Sons Boat Co. for the first few years of their new venture before being lured away by Gar Wood.

Having rubbed elbows with the rich during their racing days, the Smiths took every opportunity to get their famous friends to help show off their Chris-Crafts. Thomas Edison and Harvey Firestone, with Firestone's son Roger at the wheel, enjoy a brisk ride in a 1926 model. Note the retracted "one-man top." *Courtesy Mariners' Museum*

Though virtually all Chris-Crafts were stable displacement hulls, the company did offer a 26-foot Hydroplane in the 1928 lineup, shown here on display at the New York Boat Show. The 1928 sales brochure evoked Chris-Craft's racing heritage, noting that the step-hulled hydroplane "Baby Speed Demon, Smith-built, was the Gold Trophy winner in 1914. . . ." *Courtesy Mariners' Museum*

Two 22-foot Cadets on plane in the foreground take on two 26-footers in this 1928 publicity photo. That year the Cadet could hit 30 miles per hour powered by the new 100-horsepower Chrysler marine engine. Ventilating windshields, forward deck with a ventilating hatch, and forward hoisting rings were details the sales department felt worth mentioning. *Courtesy Mariners' Museum*

In order to stay competitive, MacKerer maintained notes comparing each of the other manufacturer's models and their retail prices. He drew up a list of all the available motors that would be potentially "suitable for runabouts," including everything from the little 235-pound three-cylinder from Pierce-Scutin Motor Company to the 12-cylinder Peerless Marine and Packard engines weighing well over half a ton.

Industry Innovations

But while the Smiths had found a measure of success in these first years of building standardized boats, with sales of 33 units ($67,642) in 1923 and 48 units ($165,485) in 1924, they knew they needed to be more efficient. They were certainly familiar with the automobile industry, and began to look for ways to apply to their modest boat-building endeavor the assembly-line approach that made Henry Ford king.

Traditionally, one group of craftsmen built a boat from start to finish. The Smiths created different stations at which workers did the same job all the time. Given that many of the company's laborers worked seasonally and were often farmers rather than fine woodworkers, this allowed them to become proficient at one element of boatbuilding. The company could maintain its standards of quality while increasing production.

This 1929 28-foot Custom Runabout *Campaigner* features the elegant upswept deck design credited to Mac MacKerer. The 28-foot Custom Runabouts were powered by the 225-horsepower Chris-Craft V-8, could hit an impressive 42 miles per hour, and sold for $4,975. *Robert Bruce Duncan*

In 1925 they more than doubled their output, shipping 111 units ($431,737), and by 1927 shipped 447 units and topped $1 million in revenue ($1,119,109). The phenomenal growth continued in 1928 when 830 units went out the boatyard gates, garnering over $2 million. It was a long way to come in six short years.

At their first national boat show appearance, the 1926 National Motor Boat Show in New York, New York, they exhibited their standardized 26-foot "Chris-Craft" runabout, now powered by a 150-horsepower Kermath that would give it its "40 Mile Chris-Craft" name.

Although they initially pushed the advantages of dealing direct with the factory in advertising, in

With a 7-foot beam and two forward and one aft cockpit, *Campaigner* has a listed carrying capacity of 11 including the driver. An 80-gallon fuel tank kept the thirsty V-8 turning the 19- x 21-inch propeller. *Classic Boating*

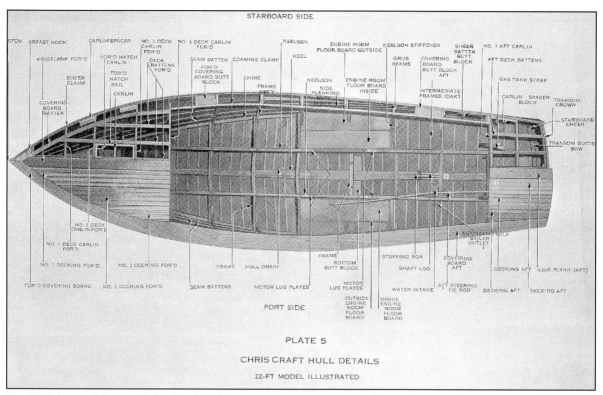

The 1929 Care and Operations Book included this description of the double-planked mahogany hulls that Chris-Craft would make famous. *Courtesy Mariners' Museum*

February 1926, four years after the Chris Smith & Sons Boat Co. was founded, the first franchised dealership was established with E. J. Mertaugh Boat Works, located in Hessel, Michigan. Mertaugh agreed to buy 11 boats. (The Mertaugh family business still exists today.) By 1930, there would be a network of more than 200 franchised dealerships.

They had help creating this stunning success from another outsider, sales director J. E. "Jack" Clifford. Clifford came to the company in 1927 from Marysville, Michigan, where he oversaw sales of the Wills Saint Claire luxury autos. Clifford would help Chris Smith & Sons create a dealer network, a New York City showroom, set up a credit plan, and improve their overall advertising and promotion considerably.

Ironically, like Nap Lisee, Clifford would also end up working for now archrival Gar Wood in the 1930s, after he was laid off during the Depression.

By 1927, the company had 26 buildings, making up a total of 2.86 acres under cover at the Algonac, Michigan, facility. They continued to look for ways to streamline the operation and cut costs. Jan Smits, service director, reported back to Sales Director J. E. Clifford on the exact dimensions of the inside of a railroad boxcar, so that they could minimize their shipping costs by maximizing the use of the space. They broke down the cost of a boat during its building, so they would know exactly how much they had invested in it at a given point. For example, by the time they had the hull framing and bottom planking in place, they'd spent 20 percent of the final cost.

Enlisting the Cadet
With a burgeoning sales network taking shape and improved production, it was time to begin broadening the product line. Joining the standardized

26-foot "40 Mile Chris-Craft" in the 1927 lineup was a smaller model, the Cadet, a 22-foot, three-cockpit runabout with a two-person front seat that made it possible to walk through to the middle cockpit (foreshadowing the 19-foot Sportsman that would come 10 years later). Designed to seat up to eight passengers, it was powered by a 70-horsepower Kermath capable of 25 miles per hour and sold for $2,250. The Cadet would be produced for three years, with options for 100-horsepower Chrysler and 106-horsepower Chrysler Imperial marine powerplants that were developed by Walter Chrysler with input from the Smiths.

But perhaps most remarkable is that Chris Smith & Sons set out to build 500 Cadets a year during an era when, as the June 1927 issue of *Motor Boating* put it, "The boat builder that had an annual production of ten boats all alike was considered to be

Interior detail of the 1929 26-foot *Cahaba*. Note the clamshell vent on the forward hatch in the deck. The 26-footers could be purchased with the 106-horsepower Chrysler six, 200-horsepower Kermath six, or the new 225-horsepower Chris-Craft V-8. *Classic Boating*

You could order your standardized Runabout any way you wanted it. For example, the searchlight mounted on the port side of the windshield wouldn't have been stock on this 1929 26-footer, but certainly could have been an option. Kermath- and Chris-Craft engine–equipped boats ran a 12-volt electric system. *Classic Boating*

doing very well. Perhaps a few built 50 boats but not more than two or three yards exceeded this number."

The magazine goes on to describe the building processes at the Algonac facility. Note the writer's use of both Chris-Craft and Chriscraft. The company used the hyphenated form at this point to describe the boats coming from Chris Smith & Sons Boat Co.

There is hardly an operation in the construction of either the 22 1/2-foot Cadet model or the 40-mile 26-foot Chris-Craft that is not taken care of by means of machinery, especially designed and built for the purpose. Even so short a time as a few months ago, it was not thought possible to eliminate many hand operations in connection

with boat construction, but Jay Smith, president of Smith Company, has worked out and had built for him machinery that eliminates practically all handwork in connection with the construction of Chriscraft.

Not long ago it took a good man the best part of the day to turn out one keel; now the stick of wood for the keel passes through a machine and the finished keel comes out in a very few moments, rabbetted, cut to length, shaped, and planed in one operation. The same is true of other major parts of the boat construction, ribs, frames, engine bed, floors, planking, transom, interior trim, bulkhead parts, seats, deck beams, and deck planking, in fact, everything is machine made and finished. A keel setup has the frames and ribs in place and is ready for the planking within hardly more than an hour. The double-planking is put on in short order by a gang of men who do no other work in the boat's construction. The lumber, screws, hardware, fittings, etc., are delivered to the men in the construction gangs in the proper amounts for each job, completely cut to size, and finished so that there will be no delay.

The mere skeleton of a hull with keel and frames set up by one gang of men moves along to the next position in the shop just the moment the last operation in connection with this part of the work is completed. This part of the boat's construction is then turned keel up and the planking operations begin. Every plank to be used for both the double-planking of the bottom and the single-planking of the boat's side has been previously cut and finished to size so that there is no fitting required and no possibility that poor workmanship at this point will later develop into a weakness. After the hull has been completely planked, it is again turned to an upright position, moved along to another position in the shop where the next force of men put in the decks, watertight bulkheads, seats, trim, etc. Then the hull moves along to the paint shop where seven coats of spar varnish are applied. This is one operation in the construction of that Chriscraft is done by hand.

Notes show that labor costs for building one Cadet in June of 1927 were $213.67, including motor installation. The "Chris-Craft" was built for little more, $235.12, in the same period. This was less than half of the labor costs MacKerer itemized for the 26-foot standardized boat prior to the improvements in production techniques, and part of the reason that the company could retail the boat for one-third less. They weren't the least expensive boats on the market, but they were fast earning a reputation for being the best boats for the money.

Marine Engine Division

The Smiths were among the pioneers of marine engine development, from Chris and his brother tinkering with outboards at the turn of the century to

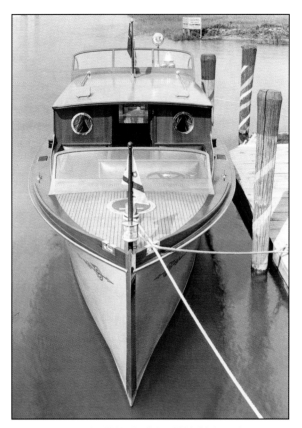

The smooth-planked V-hull of this 1929 38-foot Commuting Cruiser provided the ultimate combination of speed, smoothness, and comfort for busy executives who lived on the water. *Courtesy Mariners' Museum*

Jay and Bernard perfecting the powerplants that pushed their hulls to so many victories and world records a decade before. In order to continue their push for lower costs and better margins, and in accordance with the ways of their automotive manufacturing counterparts, it made perfect sense for the company to start its own marine engine division, announcing the first two engines in late 1927. Marine engine development had lagged behind the automotive industry, and marine engines had to withstand not only minimal maintenance and seasonal use, but needed to run at full rpm most of the time with as small a weight-to-horsepower ratio as possible. (In 1910 marine engines averaged 28 pounds/horsepower; by 1930 it was closer to 6 pounds/horsepower.)

As writer William Taylor notes in *Motor Boating* in
1930, a marine engine is "something that should drive
a parlor, bedroom and bath at any and all speeds,
with or without gas, should be built in to the hull at
time of putting on the planking and covered up and
positively kept out of sight until the planking is
removed by hitting rocks [or] sand bars due to a com-
pass that suddenly went haywire or what excuse have
you. It should not occupy space that could be used to
stow more ice and round glass containers known as
pints and quarts, or possibly a sunken garden."

Jay Smith was up to this tongue-in-cheek challenge. The first marine engines to come from Chris
Smith & Sons Boat Co. were a 150-horsepower six
and a 200-horsepower 90-degree V-8 called the A-
70. With a 5-inch bore x 5 1/4-inch stroke they displaced 825 cubic inches. The cylinders were cast in

Given the Smiths' racing background, starting their own
Marine Engine Division made perfect sense. Jay Smith, Engine
Plant Supervisor Otis Corrie, and Chief Engineer Elmer
Jasper confer in the Engine Factory while workers assemble
Chris-Craft A-120 V-8s. *Courtesy Mariners' Museum*

detachable pairs, and much of the engine was made
of aluminum. The A-70 was listed at 1,450 pounds,
or 7.25 pounds/horsepower. By the 1929 model year,
the A-70 V-8 would be listed at 225 horsepower,
available in the 26-foot Runabouts, 28-foot Custom
Runabouts, and 30-foot Custom Commuters.

Cruising Along

In 1928, Chris Smith & Sons offered 11 models,
and continued to draw on their racing history to
promote the line, evoking memories of *Baby Reliance*
("a pioneer in consistent hydroplane performance")
and "*Miss America I* and *II*, which established and still
hold the world championship record of 80.567 miles
per hour." They knew their market—those con-
sumers who already owned cars—and put forward
the slogan "The family motor car and the family
Chris-Craft are companions in transportation."

Looking to continue their remarkable innova-
tion and subsequent growth through the 1920s, the
Smiths pushed into a new market in 1928 with the
introduction of a 38-foot Commuting Cruiser.
While they had built special-order cruisers in the
past, this new model was remarkable in that it was
selling for $15,000, capable of 30 miles per hour
powered by the Chris-Craft 225-horsepower V-8.
Targeted at the upscale executive who could make a
quick trek across water to his busy downtown offices
in Chicago, Detroit, New York, Boston, or other
large city on the water, the Commuting Cruiser
offered not only the splendor of a double-planked
all-mahogany hull, but such creature comforts as
luxuriously appointed dining area, sleeping bunks,
and a galley.

And it was all working to sell boats. A list detail-
ing the board feet of mahogany used in 1928 records
that Chris Smith & Sons built 331 of the 22-foot
Cadets, 296 24-foot Runabouts, 134 26-footers, 33
26-foot Sedans, 6 28-footers, 10 30-footers, 2 of the
38-foot Cruisers, and 2 "experimental" hulls. Total
board feet used? 519,377.

The times were flush, not just for Chris Smith &
Sons but for the country. The 1929 sales brochure
pushed the luxury angle, listing among the well-
monied Chris-Craft owners names such as Astor,
Dupont, Firestone, Hearst, and Wrigley, as well as
notables such as Hollywood's Charlie Chaplin and
Count Giovanni di Sangro of Venice, Italy. The year
would see them sell 946 units for sales of more than

$3.2 million, capping a truly extraordinary decade of growth for a now eight-year-old company.

Chris-Craft (as all models were now branded) offered 18 models in 1929, ranging from the 22-foot Cadet powered by the Chrysler six-cylinder selling for as little as $2,235, to the $15,000 Commuting Cruiser. The 26-foot Runabouts stayed in the lineup with a refreshed design, and were offered with more all-weather options—from the removable "one-man top" to the Sedan models. They introduced a 24-foot (6-foot, 4-inch beam) hull available as a Runabout or Sedan, powered by the 106-horsepower Chrysler and capable of 33 miles per hour. The 28-foot and 30-foot hulls were also available, again as Runabouts or Sedans. Chris-Craft shipped 946 boats yielding $3.2 million in sales in the 1929 fiscal year ending in August.

By the 1929 model year, the boats featured a new "upswept" deck style that was incorporated throughout the runabout line. When MacKerer returned to the company after his first departure in 1925–1926, he added to his responsibilities the designer title vacated by Nap Lisee. According to MacKerer's son Don, the upswept deck runabout was one of his father's first designs for Chris-Craft and reflected some of the work he had done at Rochester Marine. "I've always thought the use and positioning of the two louvered vents and the single port on the side of the engine hatches were the secret to its overall effect" Don wrote in 1998.

As of the boating summer of 1929, hundreds of boat builders were vying for their share of an increasingly enthusiastic market. Fueled by the robust peacetime economy of the decade, many Americans had more discretionary income and more time to spend it than ever before. Thanks to Chris-Craft, Gar Wood, Dodge, Thompson Brothers, Hacker, and other boat builders, recreational boating was at a peak—some 1,424,924 motor boats were registered as of April 1930. The National Association of Engine and Boat Builders estimated that there was one boat for every 15 autos and 81 people in the United States at the time, including some 400,000 outboards. Chris Smith & Sons had, in just a relatively few years, built an empire. They, like so many others, would have never believed how quickly the market would change.

A stock 38-foot Commuting Cruiser included not only mattresses, bedding, and blankets for the four berths, but table linen, china, glassware, and silverware for the galley. *Classic Boating*

CHAPTER 2

Age of Utility

A scant eight years after the company's founding, Chris Smith & Sons' dream of creating a modern boat manufacturing facility was well on its way to fruition. They'd proven that they could build boats quickly and efficiently while meeting a high standard of quality as well as successfully reducing retail boat prices.

Though Chris-Craft "all-mahogany" inboard powerboats were still relatively expensive, the company successfully targeted the growing, family-oriented upper middle class by simultaneously promoting the exclusivity and affordability of "Chriscrafting." They were also one of the first boat manufacturers to offer a credit plan—like the auto

The Model 100 was new to the Chris-Craft lineup in 1930. The 20-foot hull had a 6-foot beam and a claimed 31 miles per hour with its 75-horsepower Chrysler six. *Sea Bee* shown here was one of a planned 500 units. *Robert Bruce Duncan*

Above: A 1939 19-foot Custom Runabout. Classic Boating

The New
Chris-Craft Fleet

The 1930 catalogue featured 24 models, "the largest and most complete motor boat spectacle ever presented." The aftershocks of the stock market crash of 1929 would not be felt in Algonac for another year—and then it would hit hard. *Courtesy Mariners' Museum*

industry, owners could buy now, pay later. As one brochure proclaimed:

> Think, then, what a Chris-Craft would mean to your family—access to the waterways of the world—thrills, luxury, convenience, comfort. Permanently it costs little if any more than the six-mile stodgy tubs—the thousands of putt-putters about the shores—yet, it glides over the waves with velvety smoothness, carries two or three families in utmost comfort.
>
> Chris-Craft is the world's finest water runabout. Two generations of boat building and testing have combined the sleekness of the Indian canoe and the

soundness of the fishing boat with the speed of the wind. In luxurious fittings and design, it vies with the smartest of motor cars. Chris-Craft is truly a prized possession one may be proud to own—proud to show anywhere, no matter what the company.

> . . . Its list of owners is a directory of directors in itself—yet new production methods place Chris-Craft definitely within reach of the average family—yes—you can afford a Chris-Craft.

According to the February 1930 issue of *Motor Boating* magazine, Chris-Craft announced "A Parade of 24 Boats" ranging in size from a "new 20-foot runabout up through the 48-foot yacht. Horsepower ranges from 75 up to 450; speed from 28 miles per hour to 45; and seating capacity from 8 to 30 persons in comfort."

The new 20-foot runabout, known as the Model 100, was reportedly on the designer's boards for more than two years, and the company planned an initial run of 500 units. With a 6-foot beam, a 19-inch draught, and the upswept deck, Model 100 used a lighter, 625-pound Chrysler six that could get the eight-passenger runabout up to 31 miles per hour. Fitted with the larger 125-horsepower Chrysler and designated Model 102, it would top out at 36 miles per hour despite the heavier (935-pound) engine.

With the successful introduction of their first cruiser the year before, Chris-Craft pushed onward, including in the 1930 lineup an impressive 48-foot Yacht powered by twin Chris-Craft V-8s generating a combined 500 horsepower. (Downdraft carburetors boosted the in-house A-70 engine to 250- horsepower spec in 1930, while keeping bore and stroke (5 x 5 1/4) the same.) Sales literature called this luxurious "express yacht" the "Flagship of the Chris-Craft fleet."

This parade of boats, the largest in Chris-Craft's still brief history, led to record-breaking sales at the National Motor Boat Show held in the spring of 1930 in New York. Initially, the stock market crash of October 1929 didn't seem to be harming boat sales. In fact, in 1930—despite the stock market horrors—Horace E. Dodge announced the planned construction of a new 100-acre plant in Newport News, Virginia, at a cost of well over $2 million, to house the Horace E. Dodge Boat & Plane Corporation.

The practical and less-expensive Utility boat was born of the tough economic times of the 1930s. *Buddy* is a 1936 17-foot Utility. *Classic Boating*

The Depression Hits Algonac

No one then, of course, could or likely would have predicted the oncoming years of the Depression. Whether you were selling cars, boats, airplanes, or houses, companies continued as best they could, believing better times were just around the corner, only to find that the worst imaginable economy just got worse.

And for the Smith family, it wasn't until late 1930 that the reality of the situation began to show on the bottom line. While they had generated more than $300,000 in profit in 1929, and had a promising start to 1930, they lost more than $100,000 in the last quarter of 1930. The Depression had hit home.

By then the 1931 sales catalog boasted that Chris-Craft offered "The Greatest Fleet in Boating History," with 37 models of Runabouts, Sedans, Commuters, Cruisers, and Yachts.

But by the end of the fiscal year in August 1931, while Chris-Craft balance sheets listed just over $1 million in assets, and sales in the 1930–1931 fiscal

Pushing beyond the 38-foot Commuting Cruiser introduced the year before, Chris-Craft offered a 48-foot Yacht powered by twin C-C V-8s in 1930. *Allez* was probably constructed in the company's new building dedicated to Cruisers. *Classic Boating*

year were $1.27 million, the company showed a net loss of $109,385.87.

In retrospect, however, the Depression helped build Chris-Craft. Before 1930, the company was one of many boat builders in America. By 1937, many of the competing pleasure-craft builders had disappeared, leaving the rebounding market open to the survivors. Jay Smith and his brothers successfully battened down the hatches by cutting back on payroll, introducing a line of low-cost Utility models, and expanding the plant during a time when it was cheapest to do so.

Not that there wasn't pain, along with the rest of America, in Algonac in the early 1930s. By the end of 1931, Chris-Craft was losing money and widespread layoffs—more than the seasonal layoffs that were common in the early years—were inflicted, affecting even the most valuable employees such as Bill MacKerer and Jack Clifford.

The 1932 catalog reflected the worsening economy—"The Greatest Fleet in Boating History" was reduced to 16 offerings: 12 Runabouts, and 4 Cruisers.

Included in the catalog was a 15 1/2-foot Runabout powered by a 55-horsepower engine selling for $795. Sales literature boasted that the first customer for this mini-Chris-Craft was none other than "HRH The Prince of Wales . . . for his personal use on his private lake at Windsor Great Park."

Chris-Craft also promoted their 1932 Runabout lineup as new "Level Riding" models, which "cut to a minimum water resistance and stern drag at high speeds." No real changes to the hulls were made, however.

The Smith family and their company survived the brutal economy in part because they could react quickly to a changing market, and in part because they carried very little debt into the Depression. But, as Rodengen chronicles in detail in *The Legend of Chris-Craft*, they also got lucky. A planned sale of stock, requiring a $250,000 nonreturnable deposit, never went through, and Chris-Craft was able to keep the deposit and use it as working capital during the leanest years. Jay Smith would say later that the windfall "saved us." The aborted stock sale, in combination with some clever accounting designed to minimize the family's tax liability, resulted in Chris Smith & Sons Boat Company being renamed the Chris-Craft Corp.

Depression-Era Chris-Crafts

Chris-Craft wasn't the only boat maker looking to make powerboats more affordable during the tough times of the 1930s. Lyman Boat Works offered 17-foot and 19-foot Utility inboards as early as 1933, and Hacker Boat Company, among others, introduced Utility models. Chris-Craft, sometimes credited for inventing the Utility, introduced its

As the power boating community matured, more customers were looking for ways to get out of the weather. This 1930s-era upswept deck Runabout features the popular one-man top. *Classic Boating*

This roomy 28-foot Custom Runabout *Birches* was originally built for families and their friends in 1931, but does equal service for the Hamilton family years later. Chris-Craft offered 37 models in 1931, but the devastated national economy would lead to a financial loss. *Classic Boating*

first Utility in 1932 (for the 1933 model year), a 24-footer that was one of just 14 models listed for 1933. It was, in essence, a stripped-down runabout built without cockpits and provided only one permanent seat; it could be ordered with either the 85-horsepower or 125-horsepower engine for top speeds of 30 and 35 miles per hour, respectively.

The ultimate low-cost Utility was Chris-Craft's Model 65, a stripped-down version of the 15 1/2-foot Runabout with tiller steering that sold for just $495 in 1935. An example remains today, owned by well-known Chris-Craft expert Dale Tassell, and is on display at the Mariners' Museum.

Customers looking to save money could also buy 18- and 21-foot Utilities, and by 1935 Chris-Craft had introduced a 25-foot Utility Cruiser for as little as $1,440.

Utilities were not just a little less costly than runabouts, however, they were also—as their name suggests—a bit more practical. Chris Smith, grandson of Christopher Columbus Smith, recalls going out with his dad, Bernard Smith, to the covered boat slips behind the Algonac factory in the mid-1930s when he was a boy. There in the boat well, as they called it, Grandpa Smith stored his 21-foot Utility

By 1934, efforts to make a more affordable boat yielded the Utility boat. This basic 15-foot Model 65 with its unique tiller steering listed for a low $495 FOB Algonac, but could still hit 25 miles per hour with its 32-horsepower engine. This rare restoration owned by Dale Tassell is on display at The Mariners' Museum. *Courtesy Dale Tassell*

outfitted with a live fish and bait well. His Uncle Jay also had a 21-foot Utility, set up with dual four-cylinder Chris-Craft engines and a right-side steering wheel. (Interestingly, the engines in Jay Smith's boat did not run in opposite directions.) Dad Bernard opted instead for the 22-foot Utility with a six-cylinder K engine and a flat windshield so that he could fold it down. Uncle Owen also had a 22-foot Utility, powered by the MB high-performance engine.

Happy Days Are Here Again

By 1935 sales were rebounding, and latter months even outperformed the sales records of 1929. Engineering and manufacturing head Mac MacKerer came back on the payroll. Wayne Pickell had been hired as national sales manager, as Jack Clifford joined the Gar Wood company after the layoff a few years earlier.

The 1936 catalog featured 66 models, the first increase in the lineup in several years. Most notably, the Cruisers were back in force, with 24 different models, including the "New Chris-Craft Clipper Cruiser." At 24 feet it was a modest Cruiser, but its 8-foot beam allowed it to sleep four, and it was capable of motoring along at 18 miles per hour. It cost a mere $1,270. A 23 1/2-foot model called the Sea Skiff was also offered. The Sea Skiff name would

NEW 19-FT. LEVEL RIDING RUNABOUT with Cockpits Forward and Direct Drive

New to the Chris-Craft fleet is this advanced design 19-ft. Runabout. Same Philippine mahogany hull, double planked bottom and batten seam side construction that have made Chris-Craft the world's standard for fine motor boats. And a revelation in design and appointments from streamlined hardware and fittings to correct balance between motor and hull for Level Riding. Complete power plant data and other specifications on pages 20 and 21.

In 1935 Chris-Craft offered double cockpit forward (of the engine) Runabouts in three lengths, 16 feet, 18 feet, and 19 feet. A contest yielded a slogan for the compact boats: "Ride Gaily through the spray; the chummy Chris-Craft way." *Courtesy Mariners' Museum*

resurface in the 1950s as the moniker for the company's lapstrake boats.

This lineup brought the company a profit of more than $200,000 in 1936, and by the end of the year, Jay Smith announced that year-round production would resume. Chris-Craft had weathered the economic storm.

The Smiths not only survived the Depression; they took advantage of it. They expanded the facilities while costs were low, adding a new office building and additional capacity in the Cruiser division. Chris, Jay, Bernard, and Owen had all experienced the cyclical nature of the boat business before, and were smart enough to put the lessons learned to good use.

Still, Chris-Craft management style was brusque. For example, in a memo dated October 14, 1936 (the company would go to year-round production that winter), Mac MacKerer complains of lights being left on after the end of the shift, writing "Apparently it cannot be left to the men themselves

Chris-Craft introduced the "Level-Riding principle" in 1932. "The new Chris-Craft develop more speed per horsepower and more speed per foot," the catalog claimed. But no amount of sales hype could jolt buyers battered by the Depression. *Phantasy III* is a 21-foot hull with a 6-foot, 5-inch beam. *Classic Boating*

By 1936 Chris-Craft was back in the black and expanding their lineup once again. *Jay Dee III* is a 1936 19-foot Special Race Boat (Model 517) and was not built for family picnics—equipped with a 155-horsepower engine, it had a top speed of 47 miles per hour. *Classic Boating*

The Chris-Craft Crest

Owning a Chris-Craft put you in elite company—even if the modest 15-foot Utility was the only powerboat in the Chris-Craft line you could afford, you shared its joys with none other than the Prince of Wales. To promote this sense of royalty, the company created a coat of arms.

At the crest is an outline of *Miss America I*, world-record setter, against a rising sun, symbolizing a rising power. The bendy, or diagonal bars at the upper left and lower right, indicates superiority among rivals, the red and silver colors convey strength, sincerity, peace, and magnanimity. In the upper right quadrant is an ancient galley, the lymphiad, an emblem of honor for acts of heroism on the sea, colored black for constancy and blue for truth. In the lower left quadrant, flying geese signify the strength and speed of the tireless goose. On the scroll below is the rallying cry, "Chris-Craft."

to take care of this. . . ." When it came to smoking in the men's room (no doubt a seriously dangerous activity in a wooden boat factory) MacKerer pulled no punches: "I have been instructed, effective Friday, Oct. 16th, to fire any employee irrespective of who he is or how long he has been in the employ of this Company that I find guilty of smoking in the washrooms. . . . The Company has been very lenient, but as is always the case—leniency breeds contempt on the part of the employees for any rules or regulations."

Six months later, with the help of United Auto Workers organizers, the plant was closed due to labor unrest. The primary issue was wages, and

Chris-Craft ultimately coughed up a 10 percent raise in hourly rates to get the workers back in the factory. Management clearly saw themselves as benefactors in a small town, while some workers felt they had to resort to work actions to be heard. Not unlike the auto industry, there would continue to be an "us-versus- them" feeling in Algonac.

The First Sportsman

By 1937, Chris-Craft was ready for the heady expansion they'd experienced in the 1920s and launched 97 different models. Included were the Utility Deluxe models, essentially 17- or 21-foot Utilities with a few extras including Linoleum floor

1936 Models 550-553 were 28-foot Enclosed Bridge Cruisers such as *Tadpole*, which were part of a growing Cruiser fleet that included the 23-foot Sea Skiff up to a 38-foot Double Stateroom Cruiser. *Classic Boating*

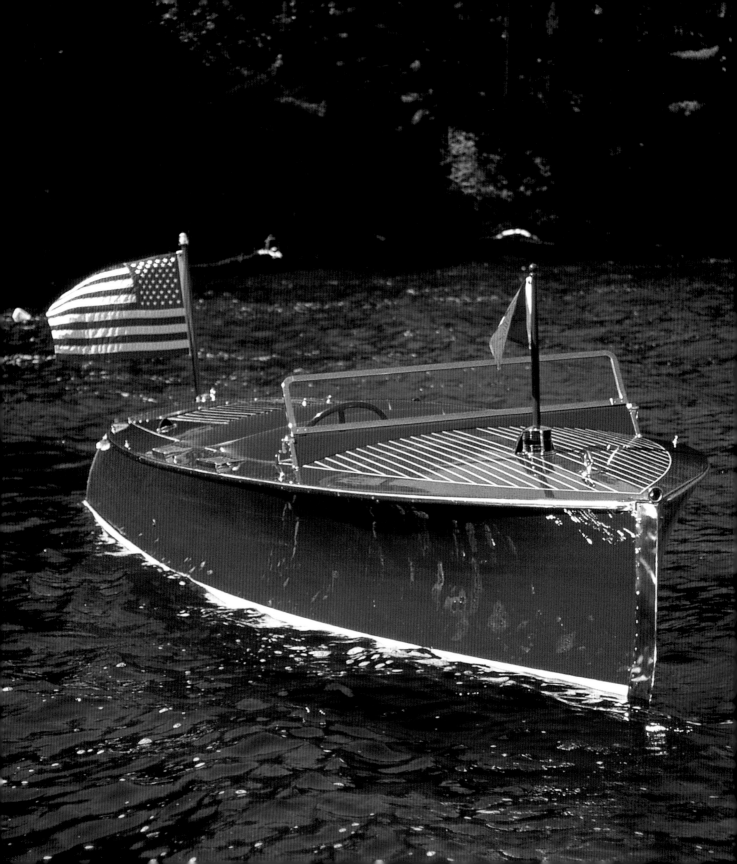

This 1937 19-foot Custom Runabout *Phantasy II* was 1 of 97 models Chris-Craft offered that year. Available with 85-, 110-, or 125-horsepower six-cylinder Chris-Craft engines, which gave it a top speed of 34–39 miles per hour, it sold for $1,550–$1,880 FOB Algonac. *Classic Boating*

covering, paneled cockpit, three-unit instrument panel, and folding windshield.

The Sportsman also first graced the Chris-Craft lineup in 1937, available with six different engine configurations (including twin 85-horsepower Chris-Crafts) and priced from $2,590 to $3,550. Not quite a Runabout and not a Utility, the 24-foot Sportsman

The 22-foot Custom Runabouts such as *Salanja* were offered with three different engine configurations, leather upholstery, and the flat folding windshield. *Robert Bruce Duncan*

tried to combine the best features of each with a stern-facing seat in the aft cockpit "specially designed for fishing, photographing, and aqua-planing . . . " according to a company press release.

For 1938, the Sportsman was also offered in a 19-foot package. Like other models, a variety of engine options were available, ranging from a 60-horsepower engine capable of 28 miles per hour to the LC 128-horsepower engine that topped off at 37 miles per hour. This first incarnation of the Sportsman did not turn out to be popular. According to research by Carl Chaverin and Bob Wright, summarized in *The Brass Bell*, a total of 70 were built from

The streamlined look overtook design in the 1930s, and boats were no exception. Chris-Craft's typical coaming disappeared, leaving flush decks and smooth lines. *Outrageous* is a 1939 22-foot Custom Runabout. *Classic Boating*

Previous pages
With enthusiastic customers clamoring for Chris-Crafts, the company opened a new plant in Holland, Michigan, where Runabouts and Utilities would be made for years to come. *Sierra Sunrise* is a 1939 19-foot Custom Runabout. *Robert Bruce Duncan*

1937 to 1939, using hull numbers 19500–19569. At least 15 of those are known to have survived and exist today, including the prototype, hull 19500.

But the Sportsman name would be revived in the late 1940s and become one of the most popular models through the 1950s' bull-nose era.

The Cruiser division continued to grow from 1938 to 1939, and the largest production model offered was upped to 55 feet. In fact, in 1939 the company created a new category for the big boats called the Motor Yachts.

Streamlining dominated industrial design in the 1930s, and Chris-Craft followed suit. As described in sales literature, "planking is narrower and thicker, transoms are more rounded . . . " The torpedo hulls, as they were known at the time, ultimately came to be called barrel stern or barrelbacks. They were almost instant classics, and turn heads as much today as they did then. The 1939 19-foot Custom Runabout, fitted with a two-piece Bugatti-style windshield, three-spoked "banjo" steering wheel, maroon leather upholstery, and six-gauge instrument panel, was the envy of many a boater.

The rebounding economy had pushed the Algonac plant to its limits, and as early as 1937 the Smiths began to search for a site for a second plant. They found it across the state in Holland, Michigan, where they purchased 23 acres in the summer of 1939. By year's end, the plant was operational, turning out 48 15 1/2-foot Runabouts before converting to its intended purpose, the production of small- and medium-sized Cruisers. Harry Coll, a college friend of Harsen Smith, was made manager of the plant, with Bernard's son George Smith on staff to lend boat-building expertise.

But 1939 is a meaningful year in the history of Chris-Craft for reasons other than new factories or new models. Christopher Columbus Smith, patriarch and namesake, passed away September 9 at the age of 78. Though he had long left the day-to-day operation of the business to his sons, preferring to while away his final years in the boiler room in Algonac, he was sorely missed. He was—and is—remembered by everyone fascinated by powerboats as a pioneer of speed and beauty on the waterways.

By 1939 Chris-Craft was again profitably dominating the pleasure boating industry as it had a decade before. *Ajax* is a 1939 19-foot Custom Runabout with streamlined barrelback stern, 1 of 115 models offered that year. *Classic Boating*

CHAPTER 3

Victory at C-C

*W*orld War II changed many companies in the United States, but few would be better prepared than Chris-Craft to meet the challenges and schedules of wartime production. Just as the Depression served to make Chris-Craft stronger, the war ultimately helped the company further dominate the marketplace even though there would be no pleasure boat construction for three years. Not only were the war years profitable, the company would add production capability and learn new technologies that would have long-term benefits once the war was over.

Though Chris-Craft was already testing Landing Craft in hopes of garnering government contracts, the 1942 lineup—including the 17-foot Deluxe *End of Watch*—was announced prior to Pearl Harbor. In the first year of U.S. involvement in the war, companies were urged to continue pleasure boat construction to keep domestic morale high. By 1943, Chris-Craft's considerable resources would be dedicated solely to the war effort. *Classic Boating*
Above: The 1946 22-foot *Water Color. Classic Boating*

By installing a high-performance 350-horsepower version of the A-120 engine, a stock V-hulled 27-foot Runabout became a 1940 Racing Runabout such as *Miss Arrowhead*. *Classic Boating*

Chris-Craft had little experience with government contracts, but as early as autumn 1940 they were testing a 30-foot Landing Boat powered by twin Chris-Craft 110-horsepower engines in competition with Higgins Industries. Though the Chris-Craft reportedly outperformed the competition, Higgins won the primary contract for 400 boats, much to MacKerer's consternation. They would get better at the politics of government procurement as the war continued.

But before Uncle Sam was dragged kicking and screaming into the conflict by the Japanese attack on Pearl Harbor in 1941, Chris-Craft continued to make pleasure boats for the American public. In 1940, they rolled out 98 models, 47 of which were Cruisers. In 1941 they upped the ante to 110 models, adding, among others, a low-priced 23-foot Express Cruiser.

Coming off a record-setting fiscal year in which sales topped $3.6 million and believing they would need additional capacity, Chris-Craft acquired land and built a new manufacturing facility in Cadillac, Michigan, where a slowing timber industry left an available skilled labor force. On February 26, 1941 (the agreement with the city of Cadillac had only been finalized on January 15), the first boat, an 18-foot Utility, had been framed.

The Cadillac plant would soon be turned over to producing 36-foot LCVPs, (Landing Craft Vehicle Personnel), ultimately delivering 2,000 of the military boats while earning the Navy's E Award for Excellence (as did the Algonac and Holland plants).

Throughout 1941, as the United States edged closer to full-scale involvement in the war, Chris-Craft was able to sell engines and stock boats to both the Army and Navy. The 22-foot Utilities were ordered for use as crash boats, for rescuing downed pilots, and several Cruisers were also sold.

As the war drew closer, civilians become more hesitant to buy pleasure boats—especially if they believed the building of their boat would take away from the war effort.

But prior to Pearl Harbor, Chris-Craft announced a 79-model 1942 lineup. Fifteen were Runabouts, including a 16-foot Special Runabout selling for under $1,000. The Sportsman was gone, but a line of six Utilities ranging from 16 to 23 feet remained. Express Cruisers (including the 40-foot Challenger), Cruisers, and 55-foot Motor Yachts balanced out the fleet. Not only would these be the last pleasure boats to be built until mid-1945, but it

The 1941 16-foot step-hulled Hydroplane was advertised as "for racing only"—the flat, *Miss America*-style bottom runs best on still waters and made Chris-Craft execs concerned about potential liability issues. Powered by a performance-tuned Model KB engine using three downdraft Zeniths and generating 121 horsepower (26 horsepower more than stock), *The Fifth* could hit 48–50 miles per hour. *Classic Boating*

would be these models that would be reintroduced and carry Chris-Craft and its loving public through the first years following the war's end.

A Winning War Effort

The first major government contract for Chris-Craft came shortly after December 7, 1941, for 1,025 Landing Boats. Additional contracts followed quickly thereafter, for building various configurations of these 36-foot plywood boats. Powered by twin engines—either 225-horsepower Gray diesels or gasoline Chryslers, LCVPs were designed to carry 36 men. LCVRs (Landing Craft Vehicle Ramp) could also carry men and jeeps.

Twin 150-horsepower Chris-Craft engines were used on another kind of boat the company built, 36-foot Navy Picket Boats. Chris-Craft would also build 27-foot hulls to be used as Army Target Boats, 42-foot Command Boats, and 60-foot Quartermaster Boats.

While Chris-Craft was positioned as well as any manufacturer to put its production-line techniques to good use during the war, they went a step further. Knowing that the war effort would make labor scarce, MacKerer and others immediately set about finding ways to further reduce the man hours required to complete a given boat. They analyzed the moving production lines, allotted a certain amount of time for each station, and investigated every excess to eliminate problems and bottlenecks. As good as they were at building good boats quickly before the war, wartime contracts made them even more efficient.

They also made the company profitable. Revenues in the 1942 fiscal year reached more than $12 million,

Chris-Craft emerged from the Depression-dominated 1930s a stronger company marketing an increasingly luxurious line to a growing upper middle class. *West Texan* is a 1941 38-foot Sedan Cruiser that was 1 of 110 models in the Chris-Craft fleet. "More beam, more freeboard, heavier construction . . . easier handling qualities and higher speeds . . ." marked the lineup according to the catalog. *Classic Boating*

and in 1943 revenues hit nearly $21 million, with similar results in 1944 and 1945. While the law limited profits during the war, Chris-Craft was able to return substantial dollars to the government due in large part to their ability to work fast and keep costs down.

While the company proudly contributed to the war effort and made a reasonable profit doing so, there were other benefits to the government contracts. Prior to building the Landing Boats, Chris-Craft had little experience with plywood. They also gained valuable experience with a new adhesive, called Thiokol. Both would prove valuable to Chris-Craft after the war as they created the Sea Skiff lapstrake-hull boat division.

Throughout the war, Chris-Craft prepared for resuming peacetime production. In 1943 the company acquired land in Grand Rapids, Michigan, and Jamestown, New York, for future plants. Advertising

Outfitted with machine guns fore and aft, a 42-foot Army Command Boat built by Chris-Craft. *Courtesy Mariners' Museum*

The LCPR, or Landing Craft Personnel Ramp could carry up to 36 men in full combat gear. Built out of plywood and powered by Gray or Chrysler engines, Chris-Craft could build the hulls faster than other suppliers could deliver the steel ramps or engines. A Chris-Craft version of these crafts was reported to be the first to hit the Normandy Beaches on D-Day. *Courtesy Mariners' Museum*

urged citizens to buy the War Bonds that would help make America victorious, and would help finance a new peacetime Chris-Craft when the war was over. "Buy U.S. War Bonds Today—Tomorrow command your own Chris-Craft" was the slogan.

And in typical Chris-Craft style, they were able to convert back to civilian models within a short time of the war's end, though as with automobiles they were primarily remakes of the early 1940s' models. The atomic bombs that forced Japan's surrender and ended the war in the Pacific led to suspension of military contracts by mid-August. Chris-Craft had already shipped their first 1946 model-year pleasure boats in late July 1945.

PreWar Styles and Painted Hulls

Among the 90 models offered in 1946 were the new Sportsman in three hull lengths, 18, 22, and 25 feet. The Sportsman class essentially took the place of the prewar Utility class boats that had become popular. Sportsman front seat backs had a center walk-through opening, which would evolve into a split front seat in 1950. The 18-footers, which remained similar from 1946 to 1954, had a varnished deck and hull, pointed bow, and modified V-windshield. Models from 1946 to 1947 were often powered by the Chrysler Ace engine.

The 22-foot Sportsman was available as an open Utility or covered Custom Sedan, and early-year models usually had white-painted cedar hulls with mahogany decks. A large fully framed windshield distinguished it from its little sister. The 25-foot Sportsman featured a double forward cockpit and sold for $4,490 with twin Chris-Craft 95-horse engines. Though "temporarily discontinued" due to wood shortages in 1947, it would be available through 1951.

Outboard Overboard

By 1949 Chris-Craft had shed the constrictions of the war and postwar years and was ready to take on new markets with new products. Among those was the new Chris-Craft 5 1/2-horsepower Challenger outboard motor. Though the market was crowded and competitive, Chris-Craft execs such as Jay Smith had long proven that they could take on anyone when they

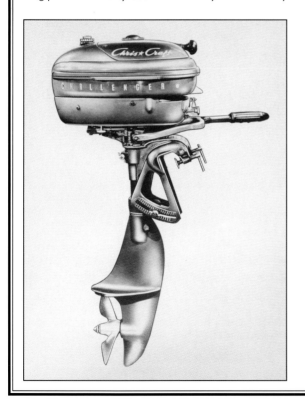

focused on giving the customer a better product at a fair price.

Manufacturing was set up in Grand Rapids, Michigan, with Harry Coll in charge—though Jay, the old engineer, led the drive to create a small two-stroke that would idle better than the competition. As they had done when they first set out to build a standardized Runabout more than 20 years before, they analyzed the best of the competition, took the best characteristics of each, and improved where they could. They ended up with a two-stroke twin with reed valves and underwater exhaust, rewinding starter, and 1 1/4-gallon fuel tank.

A year later they would add the 10-horsepower Commander outboard, while simultaneously launching their kit boat division. They seemed on the verge of yet another stunning success story.

But instead the outboard motors would become a rare misstep for Chris-Craft. The 10-horsepower Commander apparently violated a patent held by Kiekhaefer Corporation, which made the established Mercury outboards. Kiekhaefer sued Chris-Craft, and instead of fighting it, they discontinued the 10-horsepower motor and closed down the outboard operation in Grand Rapids. The 5-horsepower outboard would continue to be made by others for a number of years, but Chris-Craft pulled itself out of the outboard business.

Introduced in 1949, the 5 1/2-horsepower Challenger would be joined by the 10-horsepower Commander outboard in 1950. But a patent challenge from Kiekhaefer Corporation led to the shutdown of the Chris-Craft outboard program. Courtesy Mariners' Museum

You can expect great things from Chris-Craft after the war. Greater safety afloat. New styling . . . through new designs. Miracles of economy from war-born fuels. Greater ruggedness, more quiet operation, new comfort and conveniences from new materials. Everything in boating that is proved and practical will be incorporated in all post-war Chris-Craft.

Buy U. S. War Bonds Today—
Tomorrow command your own
Chris-Craft

Today we're 100% on war work producing vital craft for the U. S. armed forces at the fastest rate in history. Immediately after victory we'll be ready with a complete new line of Chris-Craft with models to fit every purse and purpose.

CHRIS-CRAFT CORPORATION
4000 Detroit Road, Algonac, Michigan
WORLD'S   LARGEST   BUILDERS   OF   MOTOR   BOATS

While postwar boats were based on prewar designs, the 20-foot Custom Runabout did reflect the direction of styles to come, featuring the two-tone deck and trim finish that would come to distinguish the Runabouts of the 1950s.

Many of the boats coming out of Chris-Craft following the war had painted, rather than varnished, hulls. Philippine mahogany—especially of a quality that could be called "Chris-Craft Grade," was in short supply for all boat builders. For Chris-Craft it was particularly acute since they used so much of it—as MacKerer put it in an early 1947 memo, "There should have been a shut down last Spring" due to the shortage of quality wood. (An interesting side note: the "Philippine mahogany" that Chris-Craft made famous is in fact a type of cedar, and not botanically related to Honduran or African mahogany.)

In 1942 Chris-Craft won a Navy contract to build these 36-foot Navy Picket Boats, shown ready to ship from Algonac where they were built in the Cruiser facilities. Twin 150-horsepower Chris-Craft engines gave the boats a 25-miles-per-hour top speed. *Courtesy Mariners' Museum*

By July 1945, Chris-Craft was ready to ship the first postwar pleasure boats. After three years of making nothing but war-related boats, most of the 1946 lineup was essentially a remake of 1942 models. Different, however, was the 1946 20-foot Custom Runabout with bleached mahogany finish on the king plank, cockpit trim, and engine hatch, a look that would extend to numerous models in the 1950s. The double-cockpit models proved more cost effective than the classic triple-cockpit Runabouts of an earlier decade. *Classic Boating*

Opposite
As quick and efficient as Chris-Craft was at converting to wartime production of Landing Craft and other military boats, they were equally adept at jumping back into pleasure boat production at the end of the war. As early as January 1945 they were making plans for peacetime powerboats. *Courtesy Mariners' Museum*

The wood shortages forced Chris-Craft to limit the 1947 lineup to just 21 models, including a 16-foot Special Runabout called the Rocket. Wood-hungry Cruiser models were trimmed considerably. Most hulls were painted white, including the "Red & Whites"—open-bridge Cruisers so called due to their color scheme.

Also sporting the red-and-white trim were the early 19-foot Racing Runabouts that were built starting in 1947. Designed with lower freeboard to give it the illusion of speed, these were often powered with the 158-horsepower Hercules MBL engine and were capable of 44 miles per hour—not shabby for a production boat of the day.

Wood shortages aside, Chris-Craft generated almost $6 million in sales in 1946, and more than a half million profit on $13.5 million in 1947. While it

was considerably less than the $20-million-plus total annual revenue of the war years, it compared favorably to the years just prior to the war. Chris-Craft continued to prepare for expansion, adding a Runabout production facility in Chattanooga, Tennessee, in 1946 and Caruthersville, Missouri, in 1947. And in comparison to its competitors, Chris-Craft was doing extremely well—MacKerer reported that Higgins lost $2 million in 1946, and Gar Wood Boats—which had never instituted the kind of production-line boat-building techniques that made Chris-Craft successful—would shut down in April 1947.

A New Generation

Following the war, Jay Smith's son Harsen, who had been instrumental in dealing with the government

Cruisers were in short supply in 1947, with only five lengths available, including a 40-footer such as *Ebb Tide*. *Robert Bruce Duncan*

contracts and was approaching his 40s, began to take on more responsibility for the company in place of his father. Harsen had at his side college friend Harry Coll, who would later become president of Chris-Craft when the Smith family sold the company in 1959.

Just as streamlining came into vogue in industrial design in the 1930s, eventually showing up in boats, so did postwar industrial design start changing the boats of the late 1940s and 1950s. In line with the trends of the nearby auto industry, design was divided between stylists and engineers. A naval engineer such as MacKerer would be responsible for hull design and another designer would be tasked to create a topside design that would capture the imagination of the market with input from sales.

With "Chris-Craft Grade" Philippine mahogany hard to find, the 1947 catalog featured just 21 of the most popular models, including the 26-foot Deluxe Enclosed Cruiser. A Custom Runabout is in the foreground. *Courtesy Mariners' Museum*

Starting in 1947, the first 205 (out of 503) of the 19-foot Racing Runabouts were painted red and white such as *Lipstick* (foreground). This model featured two cockpits, one fore and one aft of the engine. Most common were the 158-horsepower Hercules MBL engines, which could propel the sporty Runabout to a top speed of 44 miles per hour. *Robert Bruce Duncan*

Previous pages
As Chris-Craft emerged from the wood shortages of the postwar period, they focused on the most popular models, including this 1948 20-foot Custom Runabout. The 20-foot Customs were the first to feature a two-tone finish, with bleached mahogany king plank, rear hatch, and cockpit trim. Though similar to the Rivieras that would debut in 1949, the 20-foot Customs featured double-door engine hatches and red leather upholstery. *Classic Boating*

Chris-Craft contracted with designer Don Mortrude, who had his own design firm in Detroit and had been working with, among others, General Motors under Harley Earl. According to long-time Chris-Craft executive Larry McDonough, Mortrude probably created the new-look Chris-Craft script that showed up on the sides of the 1947 fleet. His early work for Chris-Craft probably included not only the popular Riviera but also the

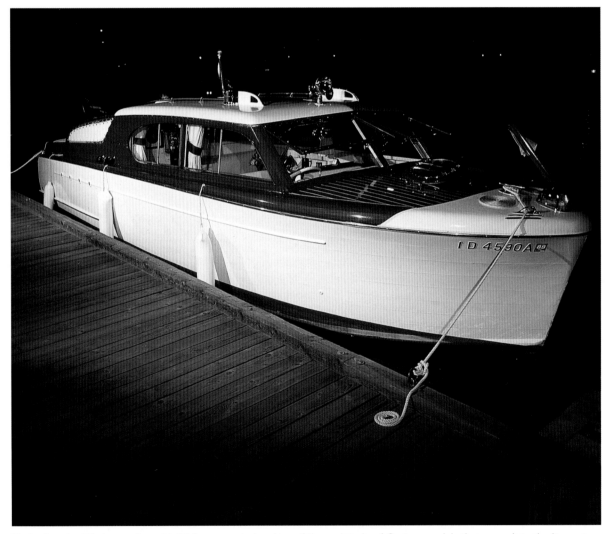

Modestly priced Sedans such as this 27-footer took the place of the multitude of Cruiser models that weren't in the lineup in 1947. Nearly all the hulls were painted in the years just after the war. *Classic Boating*

Destined to become one of the most popular models of the late 1940s and 1950s, postwar Sportsman models debuted in 1946, most with painted hulls such as this 1947 Sportsman *September II*. Like the 19-foot prewar Sportsman, these featured step-through front seats. The early 22-foot models were frequently powered by a 115-horsepower Chrysler Crown engine. *Robert Bruce Duncan*

48-foot Catalina, Commander, and Conquerer models in 1949.

In 1948, Chris-Craft had announced some 59 different models, expanding the fleet primarily through different available options. Then in 1949, the catalogue would explode with 161 different models—Runabout to Motor Yachts—with prices ranging from $1,690 to $54,800. Though World War II was over, Chris-Craft was launching its own assault on the pleasure boat market—and nobody but the competition would complain.

The 1949 lineup featured the popular and future classic Riviera, successor to the 20-foot Custom Runabout. Featuring the two-toned look of the postwar Custom, with bleached mahogany on the king plank, engine hatch, and trim around the double forward cockpit, the Riviera featured design changes that made it the precursor of the bull-nose bows of the 1950s-era Capri Runabouts that would follow.

Also debuting that year was the 34-foot Cruiser called the Commander, which would go on to become a mainstay in the small Cruiser lineup for years. Also appearing in 1949 was the big 52-foot Conqueror Motor Yacht.

And while the company was busy asserting itself once again in the inboard market, it was equally aware of the ongoing growth of the market for small outboards. The Grand Rapids facility acquired

Thirty-four foot express cruiser

Models number 40-69, -71. De Luxe Navy Top, side and aft curtains, standard.

Beauty beyond belief . . . speeds to 26 m.p.h.

during the war was the center of the development of the new Challenger 5 1/2-horsepower outboard motor. In typical Smith-family style, they had studiously researched the market, analyzed the competition, and developed what they thought would be a superior product—a twin-cylinder two-stroke that could idle better than any other engine. Harry Coll, who was instrumental in running the Holland plant, was put in charge of the Grand Rapids operation.

And though Chris-Craft sold the Jamestown, New York, facility and had a slowdown in sales in 1949, the future was rosy. The company had survived the war and had five plants in addition to the original Algonac facility—Holland, Cadillac, and Grand Rapids in Michigan, plus Caruthersville, Missouri, and Chattanooga, Tennessee. When sales literature boasted that Chris-Craft was the largest builder, it would be tough to argue the point. And no one would come close for a long time to come.

The 1948 sales brochure urged potential customers to "Make a date for '48" and featured 59 models, considerably more than the 21 models of 1947. Included among the 19 versions of Express Cruisers was this 34-footer with "chummy." *Courtesy Mariners' Museum*

After a temporary respite due to wood shortages in 1947, the 25-foot Sportsman such as *Big Red* with its 7-foot, 9-inch beam and double forward cockpit returned in 1948. Note that the forward section of the motor box is underneath the deck of the amidship seat. Available as either a single or twin screw, it was fastest when fitted with a single 225-horsepower-engine that gave it a top speed of 40 miles per hour. *Robert Bruce Duncan*

Comet, a 1948 25-foot Express Cruiser, sports the red-and-white paint scheme made necessary by the lack of Philippine mahogany following the war. Express Cruisers were available in 23-foot, 25-foot, 34-foot, and 40-foot lengths ranging in price from $3,220 to $25,000. *Classic Boating*

CHAPTER 4

Fins and Finish

*F*or Chris-Craft, the 1950s were a time of ongoing expansion, experimentation, and acquisition that would generate some of the company's most popular and most unique models. It was a period that would end in not only uprooting the company's headquarters from Michigan to Florida, but in the sale by the Smith family to a corporate owner. And though Chris-Craft would continue throughout the rest of the twentieth century as a respected brand in powerboating, it was in many ways the last decade of Chris-Craft as the first and second generations of the family knew it.

The 158-horsepower MBL engine, introduced in 1949 and 282 pounds lighter than the prewar 160-horsepower Model W, gave the 19-foot Racing Runabout such as the *Phoenix* "an honest 45 mph." In 1950, Otis Marston managed to negotiate 289 miles of the Colorado River through the Grand Canyon in a Racing Runabout. Though sand and grit in the water required prop and water pump replacements, the boat made the harrowing journey relatively unscathed, while a specially built non–Chris-Craft gave up before making it even halfway. *Robert Bruce Duncan*
Above: A 1959 40-foot Conqueror. Classic Boating

Chris-Craft Corp. growth in the 1950s mirrored the baby-boom years of the country overall. Not only did the Smith family business grow to new heights, competitors such as Owens—while only a third the size of Chris-Craft—would go from $1 million in 1953 to $12 million in sales at the end of the decade.

Like many large companies with a comfortably dominant position in their industry, Chris-Craft lost some of its entrepreneurial edge in the 1950s. The company, always good at marketing its quality product, was wary of the bleeding edge and perhaps overly concerned about taking too much attention away from the classic double-planked hulls that made the company what it was. Consequently,

Industrial designer Don Mortrude, hired by Chris-Craft beginning in the 1940s, influenced the design of the popular Riviera. The 16-footers, under-powered with the 60-horsepower four-cylinder Model B, were discontinued in 1951, but the 18-footers—such as the 1950 *50/50*—and the 20-footers continued through 1954 before yielding to the Capri in 1955. Some 1,211 of the 18-footers were made. *Robert Bruce Duncan*

competitors were able to sneak ahead in the development of fiberglass hulls.

From a design perspective, it was the era of Don Mortrude, who is credited for work on the Capris, Continentals, and Holidays, as well as the unique but short-lived Cobra and Silver Arrow. While Mac MacKerer and his staff of naval engineers would continue to do the practical hull-work, Mortrude was the stylist, creating the signature bull-nose bow, and two-toned king planks and covering boards that define the Chris-Crafts of the 1950s.

Mortrude was never a salaried Chris-Craft employee, but rather did work for hire out of his own studio. He was so closely tied to Chris-Craft through the 1950s that when the company moved its headquarters to Pompano Beach, he not only designed the building but set up shop himself across the street.

Names Not Numbers

In 1950, following the significant design and model changes of the prior year, the Chris-Craft lineup expanded to a total of 139 models, primarily multiple variations of established models. Rivieras and Sportsmen dominated the Runabout/Utility-style boats, while Cruisers dominated the lineup with 80 different versions. Included were the 34-foot Commanders and 40-foot Challengers, plus the big Conqueror Motor Yachts. Gone were the dry model number designations; it was the era of alliteration as C-words took over the Chris-Craft catalogs.

Introduced for the first time in 1950 were the Chris-Craft Kit Boats. Sold as ready-to-assemble from precut plywood, these entry-level do-it-yourself boats sold through nontraditional boat trade markets, including direct mail.

Builders of the Chris-Craft kit boats would need small, dependable outboard motors to power them, and Chris-Craft added the 10-horsepower Commander to the 5 1/2-horsepower Challenger outboard it had launched the year before. The company was clearly positioning itself to expand its reach to the low-cost end of recreational boating.

In 1951 Chris-Craft introduced 107 models, dropping the 25-foot Sportsman but including a new 62-foot Motor Yacht selling for $121,750, as well as the Holiday.

The Holiday was newly designed from the hull up, featuring stylish rounded covering boards,

The 23-foot Holiday was introduced in 1951, featuring the bull-nose bow (clipper stem) style that would characterize Chris-Craft through the 1950s. Note, too, the forward raked transom and absence of hardware on the bleached mahogany covering boards. *Classic Boating*

steeply raked and heavily chromed V-windshield and forward rake transom, all of which conveyed a sense of speed. The covering boards had no step pads, cleats, or other hardware interrupting the smooth lines, and the instrument panel was located on the bulkhead in front of the steering wheel, opposite the built-in bar forward of the passenger seat. Floorboards were made of teak.

As styled as the Holiday was, it provided the flexible practicality of a Utility boat, featuring a roomy 8-foot, 2-inch beam. Passengers could walk through the forward seat to the aft seats, which were made

possible by locating the 40-gallon gas tank under the forward seat. The Holiday was available in 19-foot and 23-foot lengths, and, powered by the 158-horsepower MBL engine, could hit 35 miles per hour fully loaded. Like the cars of its era, it was big, relatively powerful, and comfortable.

In 1952 the model lineup was similar to the previous year, and in 1953 Chris-Craft featured 111 models, including Sportsmen, Rivieras, Racing Runabouts, a slightly redesigned Holiday (to lower building costs the transom was raked aft rather than forward), and a lineup of Cruisers that

The Holiday was also available as a 19-footer such as the 1952 *Second Child* with its KLC 120-horsepower engine. Forty-gallon gas tanks under the seat gave the Holiday the openness of a Utility to go with its Runabout styling.

Below
Noisy Brown Boat is a 1953 18-foot Sportsman, featuring more conservative finish and lines than its Holiday cousin of the same year. In the background, *Foolish Pleasure* is a 1935 22-foot Custom. *Classic Boating*

Small Cruiser popularity peaked during the baby-boom years following World War II, with more than 10,000 units 21–29-feet built from 1945 to 1959. This semi-enclosed Cruiser is a 1952 27-foot model. *Classic Boating*

reflected the increasing desire for more luxurious appointments.

In 1953 Chris-Craft shut down the outboard motor plant in Grand Rapids. Not only had they invested heavily in Hercules (maker of engine blocks used in many Chris-Craft engines) the year before, but they encountered legal trouble with the 10-horsepower Commander engine and found it easier to get out of the outboard business altogether.

New Techniques, New Markets

If 1953–1954 were relatively quiet new model years, by 1954–1955 it was time to shake up the lineup

once again. Chris-Craft, putting to use knowledge gained during World War II of the sealant/adhesive Thiokol, introduced the Sea Skiff line of rugged lap-strake-hulled boats. Over the ensuing years, this line would grow to include dozens of models, from smaller 18-foot hulls to larger 40-foot models, all built at a dedicated plant in Salisbury, Maryland. Known to be dry and strong, and capable of with-standing the pounding of larger waves, the division was extremely successful.

No less consequential for enthusiasts of Chris-Craft's traditional double-planked hulls was the 1954 introduction of a Cruiser that was destined to become a long-running classic—the Constellation. At 53 feet these were serious Cruisers, powered by two or three 150- or 160-horsepower engines with cruising speeds from 18 to 24 miles per hour. The five models introduced in 1954 sold for between $42,860 and $53,560.

Also new in the Cruiser line were the 35-foot Sport Fisherman, the new black-hulled 36-foot Corvette, and the 45-foot Corsair.

Chris-Craft had been experimenting somewhat with fiberglass—using it on some hidden portions of cabins on cruisers—and in 1955 used the resin-reinforced glass fibers in the construction of one of the most radical designs in its history, the Cobra. To quote the sales literature, "This daringly styled speedster is exceptionally smooth riding at flashing speeds . . . is distinguished by its low, beamy hull of two-tone Philippine Mahogany; its raised engine cowl and tail fin with glistening gold finish; its wraparound windshield and lavishly appointed cockpit."

It was the engine cowl and tail fin that were made of fiberglass—the balance of the boat was made the traditional Chris-Craft way. The tail fin styling was reminiscent of the Ventnors introduced seven years earlier, in 1948.

Offered at either 18 or 21 feet, the single-cockpit Cobra took the place of the venerable split-cockpit 19-foot Racing Runabout. The Cobra was not a commercial success, and only 52 of the 18-footers were made, most equipped with the 131-horsepower KBL racing

Too Good for Government Work

When the Korean conflict escalated in 1950, the U.S. government came to Chris-Craft—efficient manufacturer of so many Landing Craft during World War II—for help in designing and creating a 52-foot Aircraft Rescue Boat. Meant to fish downed airmen out of the ocean, it was designed with a transom ramp that could be lowered, allowing the pilots to be brought aboard at water level rather than being heaved over one side. An underwater cage surrounded the props to keep pilots out of harm's way.

The boat had to be outfitted not only as a sort of ambulance, with a sick bay that could attend to the potentially injured airmen, but also as a firefighting vessel. An onboard pump could push streams of seawater onto flaming wreckage to aid those trying to save downed pilots.

But where the government and country were focused and all-consumed with the multiple threats of World War II, the Korean conflict only yielded frustrating bureaucracy that made meeting the government goals difficult. The design specs changed frequently; the fixed price the government agreed to pay for the 46,000-pound mahogany hulls did not. In the end, MacKerer was fuming over spending too much time,

The 52-foot Rescue Boat, designed during the Korean conflict to pull downed pilots out of the sea, involved a tricky transom ramp that dropped into the water without swamping the boat. A metal cage surrounded the props to protect those in the water. Chris-Craft would build two prototypes, but decline additional government contracts. Courtesy Mariners' Museum

effort, and money on a project with little or no return. Though Chris-Craft delivered two prototypes, and always went out of its way to help the government when it could, it declined further military contracts.

A 1953 35-foot Commander with the standard hard top. A flying bridge model with folding top was also available. *Classic Boating*

engine and capable of 39 miles per hour. A total of 56 21-foot Cobras reached the market, 21 of which left the factory with the 200-horsepower Chrysler Hemi (50-miles-per-hour top speed) and 18 with the 285-horsepower Cadillac V-8 (55 miles per hour).

Also in 1955, the entire lineup was reorganized into different series based on hull lengths. The Holiday series include 18-, 20-, and 22-foot models; the new Continental series featured 18-, 20-, 22-, and 25-foot hulls, the new Capri series included 19- and 21-foot Runabouts; the 29-foot series was the Sportsman; and the Racing Runabout series included the two Cobras. The Riviera disappeared, replaced by the Capri, which sported a wraparound Plexiglas windshield. The Continentals took the place of the upscale Holiday models that had been in production since 1951.

On the Cruiser front, the C-names continued, with the introduction of the 42-foot Commodore, which replaced the 42-foot Corvette and joined the

With engine options including 285 horsepower, the 1955 Cobra would make 55 miles per hour. Its dorsal fin styling takes a cue from the Ventnor introduced in 1948. *Robert Bruce Duncan*

Previous pages
The 21-foot Cobra features an 8-inch-wider beam and weighs 570 pounds more than the 18-foot version. Classic Boating

in Algonac. Originally founded to build tugs during World War II, Roamer became part of the growing Chris-Craft empire in 1955.

There were few changes in the 1956 lineup. The series—Sportsman, Holiday, Continental, and Capri—continued in their various lengths, while the racy-looking Cobra was discontinued. The Commander and Commodore names disappeared from the Cruiser pages of the catalog; the Constellation, Corsair, and Capitan continued; and the new 33-foot Futura—selling for between $18,960 and $22,750 depending on options—was introduced. Both the Sea Skiff and Plywood Boat Divisions grew considerably.

Commander (42 feet), Conqueror (53 feet), and Constellation (53 feet). The Motor Yachts sunk out of sight.

If these model changes weren't enough to keep Harsen Smith and family busy in 1955, Chris-Craft also started the Plywood Boat Division, which would later take on the classier Cavalier Division moniker. With kit boats selling well, and competitors such as Owens selling growing numbers of plywood boats, it was clear that a market existed for a less expensive type of boat. And given that Chris-Craft had an estimated 70 percent of the runabout market already, growth would require finding new markets.

Four mahogany and fir plywood models were presented initially, two inboard Cavaliers (15 feet and 17 feet) and two outboard Cruisers (16 feet and 20 feet). The 20-foot Gay Paree was also available in kit boat form.

The company also purchased the Roamer Boat Corporation, maker of steel-hulled cruisers, which was located not far from Chris-Craft headquarters

Goodbye Algonac

But by early 1957, Chris-Craft was on the move again—this time, literally. The Smith family, then led by Jay's son Harsen, announced that they would be relocating the Chris-Craft world headquarters to Pompano Beach, Florida. This made good business sense, they said, because of the better weather and the proximity to the growing Florida boat market. Certainly it might have been easier to attract management talent for this international business to Pompano Beach instead of the small town of Algonac. After 35 years as Chris-Craft, and decades longer as the home of a Smith-family boat company, Algonac was being left behind.

Although the Algonac plant would remain active, many Chris-Craft workers were devastated by the news. After all, the Algonac factory provided the blueprint for Holland, Cadillac, and other plants that followed. Feelings ran high—but no doubt the Smiths still remembered some of the labor actions of years past, and the us-versus-them relationship between workers and management may have made it an easier decision.

Given that the family would sell the company just two years later—in spite of Harsen's wishes—the move may have been made in part to keep happy those shareholders growing less interested in running a boat company. Or perhaps it was a calculated move to prepare the company to be sold. In any case, they bought land and built a new Y-shaped two-story Manufacturing and Engineering Center, designed by then veteran Chris-Craft stylist Don Mortrude. By November 1957, they had transferred operations.

Through the (Fiber) Glass

Pompano Beach was also the home of another boat-building company that built a small, 15-foot outboard Runabout called the Lake 'n Sea. Chris-

Chris-Craft in a Box

With Chris-Craft runabouts and cruisers dominating the pleasure boat industry, the company saw an opportunity to get a handle on the entry-level outboard market by marketing Kit boats. Not only did these relatively easy-to-assemble plywood kits introduce a generation of youngsters to wooden boats, they opened nontraditional market channels such as hardware stores, lumber yards, or direct mail to Chris-Craft Corp. First offered in 1950 were an 8-foot Pram, 14-foot Rowboat, and a 14-foot Outboard. By 1955, the Kit Boat Division was offering 28 different do-it-yourself models. Ads enticed bargain hunters with slogans such as "Own a Chris-Craft for as little as $42 full price!"

Among the variants were a 14-foot duckboat reminiscent of Chris Smith's earliest efforts (introduced in 1953), the 12-foot Penguin

Chris-Craft's Kit Boat Division, first launched in 1950, found an enthusiastic market for low-priced do-it-yourself boat projects such as this 1956 14-footer, White Lightning. Though the kits were discontinued in 1958, Chris-Craft continued to receive orders well into the 1960s from customers reading ads in out-of-date magazines such as Boy's Life.

(Chris-Craft's first sailboat), small outboard runabouts with enticing names such as Zephyr and Hornet, and even a 31-foot Express Cruiser that would challenge most average hobbyists.

The division even reached beyond the strictly boating arena, offering kits for a 14-foot camping trailer called the Chris-Craft Land Cruiser, and a gun cabinet.

By 1958 Chris-Craft's Cavalier plywood boat division was well established, providing numerous entry-level models that competed with the kit boats. The Kit Boat Division was eliminated, inventory sold off through 1959, and the build-your-own Chris-Craft era came to an end.

001 is a 1955 Capri, introduced that year to take the place of the popular Riviera. Two lengths made up the Capri series, 19 and 21 feet. Equipped with a 200-horsepower engine option, the 21-foot model could hit 49 miles per hour and sold for $6,030. *Robert Bruce Duncan*

Below
The 1955 Capri is distinguishable from its Riviera predecessor by its wraparound windshield and the steep rake of the bull-nose bow. *Classic Boating*

Craft purchased the company because the Lake 'n Sea was made with fiberglass, which was beginning to look like it might play a large role in the future of small pleasure boats.

Unfortunately, the Lake 'n Sea fiberglass and plywood combination had not yet been perfected. The fiberglass would separate from the plywood, allowing water to further delaminate the 'glass, and the Lake 'n Sea quickly became known as the "Leak 'n Sink." Discouraged, Chris-Craft sold the company.

Elsewhere, however, business was good. In general, the 1957 Chris-Craft lineup followed on from 1955 to 1956, with Sportsmen, Holidays, Continentals, Capris among the Utility/Runabout line, and Constellations, Commanders, Futuras, Corsairs, and Conquerors among the Cruisers. A Motor Yacht reappeared, the luxurious 56-foot Salon, meant to be a floating living room.

The Roamer steel boat division offered 28-foot and 35-foot models, selling for $12,380 and $21,840, respectively. The Cavalier Division offered 27 different models of plywood boats, including Utilities, Runabouts, and Cruisers in both outboard and inboard configurations. Some 61 models of the round-bilge lapstrake Sea Skiffs could be ordered in hulls ranging from 18 to 40 feet.

Automotive styling cues continued to flow from the design-pen of Don Mortrude into 1958

Looking to expand their market beyond traditional boat dealers, ads such as these ran in popular magazines throughout the 1950s. Boats, gun cabinets, even a Chris-Craft Camper—Chris-Craft sold them all to enthusiastic customers. *Courtesy Mariners' Museum*

Lessons learned about the sealer/adhesive Thiokol (AKA "Chris-Craft Sealer") during the war helped the company when it came to starting the new Sea Skiff Division, which built lapstrake hulls such as *Happiness Is*, a 1956 Sea Skiff. *Classic Boating*

with the introduction of the unique Silver Arrow, the "sports car of the waterways" that featured tail fins and a very carlike dash and forward deck. Like the Cobra in 1955—and despite the ill-fated Lake 'n Sea fiasco—the Silver Arrow used fiberglass as well as planked spruce and mahogany. Unlike the Cobra, the fiberglass was more than top dressing. The sides of the hull were fiberglass-reinforced spruce, and the decks were molded fiberglass.

There's been considerable debate about the role of the Silver Arrow as Chris-Craft's initial foray into fiberglass hulls. From a sales perspective, the boat

As other models came and went, the Constellation cruised onward toward its status as a popular Chris-Craft classic, including this 1956 38-foot model. *Classic Boating*

Chris-Craft in the Movies

Gleaming mahogany cutting cleanly and powerfully through crystal waters makes a pretty picture, so it's no wonder that Chris-Crafts have garnered the attention of Hollywood. Perhaps the most famous Chris-Craft cameo was *Thayer IV*, a 1950 22-foot Sportsman with hull number U22-1802, that starred in *On Golden Pond* with Henry Fonda and Kathryn Hepburn. Several like boats were used in filming, and two are now kept in Florida at a Key Largo hotel.

Chris-Craft movie stars include no less than the King himself, Elvis Presley, whose *Easy Come, Easy Go* featured a Cruiser. Another Cruiser was featured in *Assault on a Queen* starring Frank Sinatra, as was a 45-foot Corsair in *The Russians are Coming, The Russians Are Coming*. Rivieras were included in Jerry Lewis and Dean Martin's *You're Never Too Young* as well as in the Bruce Willis action flick *Striking Distance*.

Like the "U-22" made famous in the movie On Golden Pond, Baby Ruth *is a 1950 Sportsman. Its conservative styling is a throwback to the prewar years.* Classic Boating

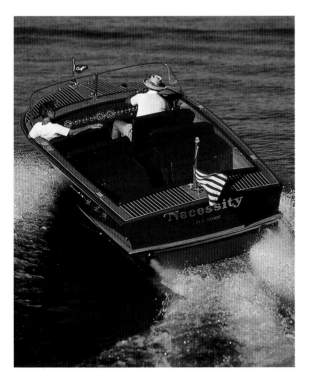

The roomy Continentals, such as this 1957 model with twin six-cylinder engines, were introduced in 1955, replacing the Holiday as the top-of-the-line offering in the line-up. Classic Boating

Left
The clipper stem (raked forward), also called a bull nose bow and characteristic of the 1950s-era Chris-Craft styling, in profile on a 1956 23-foot Continental, *Splish Splash.* Robert Bruce Duncan

By 1957 the Plywood Division had taken on the Cavalier name of its popular model, such as this 1958 15-foot Cavalier *Little Chris*. *Classic Boating*

The moderately priced plywood Cavaliers sold well enough to make the Kit Boat Division extinct. Cavaliers used mahogany and fir plywood, and Chris-Craft applied its usual high standards in obtaining quality marine "Chris-Craft Grade" materials. *Classic Boating*

was less than successful—92 of the 19-footers were delivered during the two years of production. That lackluster performance may have turned Chris-Craft prematurely away from the fiberglass future that was but a few years away.

But some have maintained that by creating a fiberglass boat, industry-leader Chris-Craft opened the floodgates for competitors by figuratively stamping the new material with a Chris-Craft seal of approval. Others, however, have suggested that Chris-Craft was too timid—insisting on a fiberglass shell around a traditional planked hull, yielding an overweight (600 pounds more than the same-length Capri), expensive boat that turned its potential customers away—perhaps to the up-and-coming competition.

Of course, the Silver Arrow was not the only boat in the 1958 Chris-Craft lineup that featured a fiberglassed hull. The plywood Cavaliers were offered with a fiberglass-covered bottom as an option.

Regardless, the Silver Arrow is now a rare classic. It was originally offered with either the KBL

Sporting automotive-style tail fins, the 19-foot Silver Arrow was introduced in the 1958 Chris-Craft lineup. Fiberglass encased a traditionally planked hull, making for a heavy, expensive boat relative to its sister Runabouts. *Jake* is a 1959 model—only 92 Silver Arrows were delivered in two years of production. *Robert Bruce Duncan*

Below
The automotive influence of the Silver Arrow's styling extended to the dash and hoodlike fiberglass deck. Since the boat was meant to be appropriate for water-skiing, the ensign pole holder doubled as the fitting for the ski tow ring. *Classic Boating*

131-horsepower engine, giving it a 36-miles-per-hour top speed, or the 215-horsepower Dearborn Interceptor that pushed it up to 40 miles per hour. It listed for $5,290, seated five, and weighed 2,770 pounds. (The 18-foot Holiday sold for $3,940, seated six, and at 2,170 pounds could hit 37 miles per hour with the KBL 131-horsepower engine.) And in a sense, it was a nearly perfect metaphor for Chris-Craft at the end of the 1950s: Despite modern styling and the appearance of speed, underneath was a double-planked hull much like those built when the Chris Smith & Sons Boat Company started in 1922. The question was, did the Smith progeny have the energy to take the company into a new era of boatbuilding?

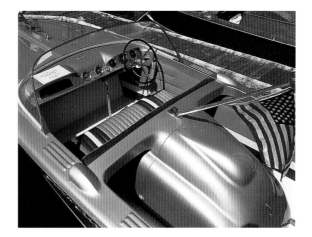

CHAPTER 5

Vinyl and 'Glass Prevail

*C*hris-Craft was at the top of its game in the late 1950s. With nine plants manufacturing more than 8,000 boats a year, it generated $40 million in sales and dominated its market. The Chris-Craft name was known far and wide for quality and value in pleasure boats. Omnipresent in the boating press, Harsen Smith, who had been in the business his entire life and was then chairman of the board, even made the cover of Time *magazine as a part of an article on "The New Boom in Boating" in the spring of 1959, in which he was credited as "The man who perhaps more than any other put the U.S. family afloat...."*

The varnished brightwork of a mahogany hull such as that of *Anticipation,* a 1959 18-foot Continental, would become rare in the 1960s and then ultimately disappear as fiberglass construction took over the pleasure boating industry. The Smith family—perhaps foreseeing the end of an era—sold Chris-Craft in early 1960. *Robert Bruce Duncan* Above: A 1960 36-foot Cruiser. *Classic Boating*

As part of a redesign under the new ownership, Sportboats such as this 1962 Holiday featured white vinyl fore decks, and interior side panels and flooring instead of the traditional varnished mahogany, with a black, gold, and white color scheme. The bow was severely raked and extended spray rails adorned the aft sides. The sleek look left little doubt that a new leadership team was in place at Chris-Craft. *Classic Boating*

Heady stuff for a family business with modest beginnings. But changes were fast approaching. In 1958, Harsen named Harry Coll—his old college friend who had been with Chris-Craft since 1939 and served as manager of the Holland plant, the outboard motor plant in Grand Rapids, and later as president of the acquired Roamer Division—president of the Chris-Craft Corporation.

Shoving Off

Less than a year after Harsen was on the cover of *Time*, Chris-Craft was sold. When the Smith family

Thought to be the last wooden Runabout built by Chris-Craft, *Miss Mohawk* left the Cadillac plant in the summer of 1961, the last year of the Capris. (Wooden utility-style Sportboats and Cruisers would linger on for a few years yet.) The 19-footer was powered by the Chris-Craft converted Chevy 283-cubic-inch V-8 making 185 horsepower and propelling the Double Cockpit Forward Runabout to a listed top speed of 40 miles per hour. *Classic Boating*

decided to sell Chris-Craft to National Automotive Fibers, Inc. (NAFI) in 1960, it seemed to come about almost serendipitously, with a chance meeting at the New York Boat Show leading to a relatively quick sale.

But in hindsight, the sale seems as carefully planned as any Chris-Craft construction line. Chris-Craft Corp. used its strong cash position to hold onto its dominant market share and grow by acquisition throughout the 1950s. The early shareholders—Jay, Owen, and Bernard—were getting older. Technology was threatening to make the traditional product the family loved obsolete, and re-tooling for fiberglass would require a major overhaul.

The company moved its world headquarters away from the traditional home in Algonac to Pompano Beach, then installed the first non-family-member president in the history of the company. Always good at publicity, the company's chairman of the board made the cover of *Time* as part of a highly flattering article. If ever you wanted to get top dollar for a business, this would be the way to go about it.

Jay, Owen, Bernard, and Harsen were trustees for others of the 55 family members who owned stock. As the story goes, Owen, 61, who still had 20 percent of the stock—more than any other family member—wanted to sell. Others did not—especially Harsen, who like his father and uncles literally grew up messing about with Smith family boats. Initially they considered taking Owen's share public, with most of the rest of the family holding. But when the company was valued at $45–$50 million, it wasn't hard for other family members to agree with Owen. The word was put out that for the right money, Chris-Craft was for sale. Brunswick-Balke-Collender Co. and Singer Manufacturing Co. were both interested.

But, according to a *Business Week* article from May 1960, Owen met up by chance with a representative of Shields & Co., owners of NAFI, at the New York Boat Show in January 1960. Owen prepared the Shields brothers, Paul and Cornelius, for a meeting with Harsen, and within a month—February 7—Harsen and the Shields hammered out an agreement to sell to NAFI for $40 million, and the Smith era of Chris-Craft was over. Harry Coll continued on as president of the company, while Harsen left to manage the family's trust made up of proceeds from the sale.

New Designs on Mahogany

The 1959 model year saw the end of the fiberglass-encased Silver Arrow, and a slimmed-down lineup of 72 traditional Chris-Crafts, plus the steel-hulled Roamers, plywood Cavaliers, and lapstrake Sea Skiffs. Notable was the introduction of the 17-foot Ski Boat, a model that would continue into the 1960s and the subject of growing restorer interest today.

Looking ahead, Harry Coll set out to spice up Chris-Craft design, creating an in-house styling group reporting to Mac MacKerer—including Fred Hudson, who was recruited from Chrysler—to begin working on the Cavalier, Sea Skiff, and Roamer Divisions. Soon after, the new group's ideas displaced Don Mortrude, who had influenced the styling of the 1950s. A new era of Chris-Craft design was about to be unveiled.

And with the sale of the company came a determination to rework the Chris-Craft lineup. For those now in charge, that meant a move away from the mahogany brightwork that had been Chris-Craft's signature look for 40 years. To the speed-hungry powerboat enthusiast of the early 1960s, Chris-Craft's traditional varnished Runabouts and Utilities may have looked dated and slow compared to flashier fiberglass-and-vinyl competitors. The American muscle car was coming into its own, confirming the market's thirst for horsepower. By 1962, the new owners of Chris-Craft reworked the speedboat line considerably.

With severely raked bows and square transoms, white vinyl-covered decks, interior side panels and flooring, and a new

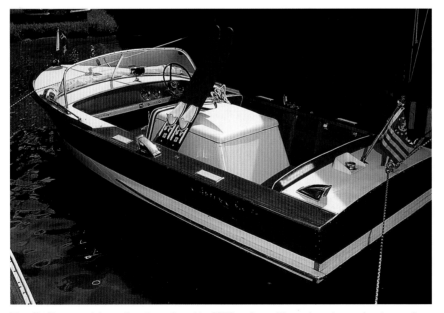

The Ski Boat model was first introduced in 1959 and would continue in production under NAFI ownership through 1967. By 1963, vinyl covered the decks and engine cover of this utility-style Sportboat, which was often powered by the flywheel forward Chevy 283-cubic-inch V-8s. *Classic Boating*

black, gold, and white color scheme, this was a considerably different look from the Capris and Holidays that dominated the previous decade. The number of models offered by the Chris-Craft Division was pared down in 1960 (44) and again in 1961 (37). The 32-foot Commander was discontinued, leaving a version of the Constellation line to fill the small cruiser niche.

Meanwhile, the Roamer, Sea Skiff, and Cavalier fleets were continuing to grow in importance to the company. Steel-hull construction costs had dropped and could rival the cost of mahogany. Fiberglass was gaining. The traditional mahogany Chris-Craft was an endangered species—and in fact the Capri Runabout would be dropped from the lineup after 1961.

Along with new designs came re-energized sales initiatives. To bolster European sales, the company opened an office in Switzerland in 1961 and a manufacturing facility in Fiumicino, Italy, in 1962.

New Boats, New Customers

The impact of these new directions would be seen by the public in 1962 with sleeker versions of the Holiday, and the introduction of what would be a commercially unsuccessful 16-foot Ski-Jet. This jet boat used a Buehler Water Jet Propulsion unit together with the 185-horsepower V-8 to reach 43 miles per hour, but with the price at $4,595, less than 50 were built before the model was dropped in 1963.

Reworked lineups in the Cavalier and Sea Skiff Divisions also showed up in 1962, and Roamer began making an aluminum-hulled Cruiser called the Comet.

No less important was the 1962 purchase of Thompson Boat Company of New York, which had made modest progress in building 16- to 20-foot fiberglass outboard runabouts and cruisers. It was a fast way to ramp up Chris-Craft's fiberglass development, and research continued apace at a brand-new R&D facility opened at the Pompano Beach headquarters that year.

Thompson, based in Cortland, New York, also had experience with Volvo's Transdrive, or in/outboard, engines. Among the advantages of this powerplant configuration was making boats more easily trailerable.

Chris-Craft worked with Thompson to create and launch later in 1962 the Corsair lineup of fiberglass Runabouts and Cruisers powered by outboards or the Volvo Transdrive.

With the addition of a Canadian facility in Stratford, Ontario, in 1965, Chris-Craft had nearly 2 million square feet of manufacturing space—plenty of room to build this 1965 65-foot Constellation *Pizzazz. Classic Boating*

The Super Sports

By 1964, the year of Ford's Mustang, it was time for more model changes in the Chris-Craft Division. The 17-foot Ski Boat had been added in 1963, joining the 18- and 20-foot Holiday and 21-foot Continental, all powered by the 185-horsepower V-8. But with the market's interest in power, Chris-Craft once again took a page out of the automotive marketing manual and introduced the new Super

By 1964, fiberglass construction was threatening the Cruiser lines, as an all-fiberglass 38-foot Commander was introduced in 1964. The venerable Constellation line would hang on for another eight years. *Pathfinder* is a 1964 57-foot Connie, which was also available that year in lengths of 27, 30, 34, 37, 42, and 52 feet. *Classic Boating*

Sports, performance-oriented 18- , 20- , and 21-foot utility-style powerboats made for speed.

Using the same hulls as the other Sportboats, Chris-Craft put together a high-performance package that helped the Super Sports not only outsell their sister craft the first year but forced the Holidays and Continental out of the lineup by 1965. Instead of the serviceable 185-horsepower engine (the 18-foot S/S did offer it as an option), the Super Sport package included either a 327-cubic-inch or 430-cubic-inch V-8 making 210 or 275 horsepower, respectively. Also part of the package were a streamlined racing rudder, super-speed cup prop, and Super Sport emblems on the hull sides and on the dash.

The Fiberglass Revolution

Still, the Super Sports were wooden boats, and it was a fiberglass future that induced Chris-Craft to introduce that same year a 38-foot all-fiberglass

Cruiser, the Commander. The largest-production fiberglass boat built to that point, it was promoted as the breakthrough that would put Chris-Craft back in the pilot's seat of the boat technology race.

The Commander, powered by twin V-8s, sold for just under $30,000, making it competitive with similarly equipped wooden Cruisers in the Chris-Craft and Sea Skiff fleets. Subtract the maintenance required of a wooden hull, and it was a bargain. Within a short time the company established a Commander Series Fiberglass Division and began adding models, including the Sport Fisherman and smaller (27-foot) Commander powered by a single 210-horsepower V-8, slept four, and sold for just under $10,000.

Raising the Sail

Although Chris-Craft's owner, NAFI, was in the automotive parts business, the influence of avid, competitive sailor Cornelius Shields of Shields and

Company, major stockholders, was bound to make itself felt. Just two years after the sale, the company let the world know that they would be entering the sailboat business. The fiberglass sailboat business.

First on the drawing boards was a 35-foot Sail Yacht, or Motor Sailer. Designed by Sparkman & Stephens, it used a reinforced fiberglass hull and included an inboard 60-horsepower Chris-Craft engine. No doubt as NAFI retooled Chris-Craft to make it competitive in the fiberglass boat market, the Motor Sailer played a key role in research and development.

In 1964, a 30-footer called the Capri was introduced, using the recognizable name of the Capri Runabout made defunct only two years earlier. In 1965 the 30-foot Shields One-Design debuted—it was essentially a sailboat for stock racing. By 1968, Chris-Craft had a lineup of eight different sailboat models, adopting American Indian names such as the Cherokee 32, Apache 37, and the queen of the sailing fleet, the 42-foot sloop Commanche 42.

But with the takeover in 1967, enthusiasm for the sailing market waned, and the lineup dwindled back down to the original 35-footer, then called the Caribbean 35. By 1976, Chris-Craft's owners withdrew from the sailing market.

The Siegel Years

The next era of Chris-Craft ownership and direction docked in Pompano Beach somewhat uninvited, as Herbert J. Siegel engineered a successful takeover in late 1967. Siegel, who moved the corporate headquarters of what was then Chris-Craft Industries, Inc., to New York, also separated the Boat Division from the rest of the corporation's interests.

In 1968, there were 14 models in the fiberglass Commander line, and only 11 models of planked mahogany boats. Sea Skiffs had dwindled to 8 models and Cavaliers to 10 models. Included among the traditionally constructed boats were the Super Sport version of the 17-foot Ski Boat, 17- and 20-foot Grand Prix models, Constellations in

With avid sailor Cornelius Shields a major stockholder in the 1960s, Chris-Craft looked to enter the sailboat market with 35-foot sloop-rigged Sail Yachts. These fiberglass-hulled Motor Sailers included a 60-horsepower Chris-Craft engine and sold for $25,790. By 1968 Chris-Craft would have an eight-model lineup, but by 1976 they pulled the plug on sailboats. *Courtesy Mariners' Museum*

six lengths from 30 to 65 feet, a 36-foot Corvette, and a Motor Yacht.

The trend continued in 1969, when the company introduced a 60-foot fiberglass Commander Motor Yacht. Even the biggest boats of the fleet were overcome by the advantages of fiberglass.

It was, in so many ways, the end of an era. Mac MacKerer had retired in 1965, after more than 40 years of working with Chris-Craft. Harry Coll stepped down as president in October 1969, replaced by James Rochlis, previously president of the Industrial Division. In late 1969, the company not only moved the Engine Division to Gallipolis, Ohio, but by mid-1970 had closed the production plant at Algonac, Michigan. The Parts Division remained, but the last boat to leave Algonac, according to Rodengen's *The Legend of Chris-Craft*, was a 46-foot Aqua-Home houseboat in March 1972.

From a marketing standpoint, the company was mindful of the value of its mahogany heritage. It staged a contest to find the "Oldest Living Chris-Craft" in 1969, ultimately christening *Miss Belle Isle* the winner. The 26-foot standardized Runabout from 1923 was restored, including the 90-horsepower Smith-Curtiss OX-5 converted aircraft engine, in Algonac. *Miss Belle Isle* was eventually donated to the Mariner's Museum in Newport News, Virginia, where it is still on display.

Running Out of Gas

With an uncertain economy, the 1970 lineup was narrowed still further. The 17-foot Ski Boat survived among the fiberglass Lancers in the Sportboats. The Cruiser models of the Chris-Craft, Cavalier, and Sea Skiff wooden boat Divisions were combined and offered just six models including the never-say-die mahogany Constellations.

In 1971 Chris-Craft purchased Gull Wing, makers of trailerable 16- and 19-foot fiberglass tri-hulls, from the Outboard Marine Corporation. While the mahogany Constellations hung on, the Chris-Craft lineup became more generic.

And then, finally, in 1972, the last wooden boat would be made. Pro football commissioner Pete Rozelle, one of the directors of Chris-Craft Industries, Inc., took delivery of a 57-foot Constellation.

The 1970s were not kind to many industries, and powerboating was no exception. The Chris-Craft Boat Division, as one part of a diverse corporation, suffered not only from the economy and the oil crisis, but from corporate issues that had little to do with producing and selling boats. The energy crisis that helped make muscle cars extinct hurt powerboating considerably. The stagnant economy led to some of the most unprofitable years in the company's history—it would lose more than $5 million in 1975 on sales of under $40 million, and lost nearly $5 million again in 1976.

As a consequence, cost cutting was the watchword for the mid-1970s. The Chattanooga, Tennessee, Sportboat plant was closed and consolidated with the Holland, Michigan, plant. The Italian plant was closed in 1978.

A Turnaround Begins

By 1978, the Chris-Craft Boat Division was still posting losses, and corporate chairman Siegel installed turnaround specialist Richard Genth as president. An ocean racer and former test pilot, once again Chris-Craft had someone who knew boats—albeit small Sportboats and not the Cruisers that made up so much of the Chris-Craft line—at the helm.

Genth moved quickly, converting the Holland plant to exclusively Cruiser production and opening a facility in Bradenton, Florida, dedicated to a new line of Scorpion Sportboats. Convinced that the Pompano plant, where the largest aluminum Motor Yachts were produced, was costing money, Genth closed it in 1979, moving administrative headquarters to Bradenton. The Engine Division in Gallipolis, Ohio, was spun off from the Boat Division.

Chris-Craft was left with just two plants, Holland and Bradenton. With these moves, and renewed sales enthusiasm, Chris-Craft managed to post a modest profit in 1979. Not surprisingly, this made the still well-regarded and well-known company ripe for a sale.

The Murray Years

It was G. Dale Murray, along with Genth, lawyer F. Lee Bailey, and Walt Schumacher, who ended up buying the Boat Division from Chris-Craft Industries, Inc. for $5 million in December 1981. They acquired the Holland plant, the Bradenton plant, licensed the Chris-Craft name from the Corporation, and would be known as Murray Chris-Craft. Murray would begin again the cycle of acquisition to build the company's revenues and market share.

The stalwart Constellation, such as the 1965 *Summer Classic*, would carry the double-planked mahogany hull tradition to the bitter end. Pro football commissioner Pete Rozelle, a member of the Chris-Craft Industries Board of Directors in the late 1960s and 1970s, purchased the last wooden boat, a 1972 Constellation, from the Holland plant. *Classic Boating*

In spring 1983, Murray purchased the Viking Boat Company in Indiana, makers of tri-vee hulled Sportboats, and renamed it Murray Chris-Craft Sportdecks. Murray and Genth worked together to introduce new lines of Sportboats and Cruisers.

Sales spiked as the postrecession 1980s replaced the malaise of the 1970s. Revenues in 1982 jumped to $55 million, then jumped again in 1983 to nearly $95 million, and again in 1984 to more than $125 million. Murray got out his checkbook again and bought Uniflite in 1984 in order to add manufacturing capacity.

Traditions Return

Among the promotions that fueled this success was a move by the company to reach back to the traditions of the Smith family's early years (and Genth's passion) and into the offshore racing scene. Murray Chris-Craft recruited former world champion Don Pruett to lead the effort. Pruett commissioned catamaran designer George Linder to design what would be called the Chris-Cat, a high-performance catamaran hull. It would set a Class II national speed record in 1984, and capture the APBA modified-class world championship in 1985. Then, in 1985, a Chris-Cat

Change was once again the watchword as Herbert J. Siegel led a successful takeover of Chris-Craft in 1967. By this time the metal-hulled Roamer division had appropriated the Riviera name for models such as this 1967 37-footer. *Classic Boating*

driven by Jack Bishop set a new world speed record of more than 116 miles per hour for the modified class. The Drug Enforcement Agency would buy six Chris-Cats to use against drug smugglers, an echo of Prohibition days earlier in the century.

Less successful was the partnership between Genth and Murray. Genth left in 1984 and would end up purchasing Donzi Marine with veteran Chris-Craft advertising executive C. Gordon Hauser. Ernest Schmidt took over for Genth at Murray Chris-Craft, and in 1986 Murray named Bruce J. Donaldson, who had been first hired by Harsen Smith, president and COO.

As the booming economy of the 1980s continued, the company restored other vestiges of Chris-Craft's past. Like the Smiths' early years, when they were able to parley their connections to the rich and famous into prestige for the boats they built, Dale Murray had on his board of directors and rubbed

elbows with *Tonight Show* co-host Ed McMahon, Alexander Haig, and others. Cruisers made a comeback, including the reintroduction of the Constellation name. The Cavalier name also resurfaced, attached to 17- to 19-foot Sportboats.

Along with the nod to the past, Murray Chris-Craft also developed new models, including the Amerosport line of sleek, high-tech express cruisers, introduced in 1987. The high-performance Stingers and the Scorpions introduced by Genth continued, supplementing the popular Limiteds and the entry-level Cavalier Sportboats. With revenues nearing $200 million, Chris-Craft was once again a leader in pleasure boating.

But like other high-roller investors of the 1980s, Dale Murray's luck would run out. Brunswick Corporation, owner of Mercury Marine, went on a buying spree, adding Bayliner and Sea Ray to their portfolio in 1986. Needing capital to compete with the mono-lith created by the Brunswick acquisitions, Murray brought Saudi Arabian investor Ghaith Pharaon on board with Murray Industries. Pharaon had majority interest in the boat company, and in 1988 Murray's execs were ousted.

The complicated ownership situation made cash flow difficult, and Murray filed for Chapter 11 bankruptcy protection. In an auction held in a Tampa, Florida, courtroom in February 1989, Outboard Marine Corporation acquired Chris-Craft for $53 million.

OMC, itself a company with a long history in recreational boating, has been a responsible steward of the Chris-Craft legacy through the century's last decade. The cycle of retrenchment and rebirth continued, as the boating industry suffered through the deep recession of the early 1990s. The Chris-Craft lineup, as it had been in the 1930s, 1940s, and 1970s, was whittled down to the most profitable models, then relaunched with redesigns and refinements. And as we enter the twenty-first century, there's no reason to doubt that—as the faithful have always said—"there will always be a Chris-Craft."

By 1967 the move to fiberglass was well on its way, with only 11 traditional mahogany models left in the Chris-Craft lineup of Sportboats, Cruisers, and Motor Yachts. Included was the 17-foot Ski Boat, which, along with two lengths of Grand Prix, were the only mahogany Sportboats left. *Classic Boating*

Resources

Chris-Craft Archival Collection
The Mariners' Museum

The Mariner's Museum in Newport News, Virginia, houses the vast Chris-Craft Collection, the paper records of the Chris-Craft company from 1922 to 1980. The collection includes not only thousands of photographs and most of the resources referenced in this book, but most of the nearly 100,000 hull cards.

For Chris-Craft boat owners wanting to get as much background as possible on a specific boat, the starting point is to identify the hull number. From the hull number, the research staff at the museum can prepare a research package that includes the boat equipment record (hull card), copies of sales literature, the original price sheet, black and white photo, engine information, and lists of the technical drawings and wiring diagrams that are available.

Locating Your Hull Number

On Chris-Craft, Sea Skiff, and Cavalier Division boats, the first place to look would be on a metal plate attached to the underside of the engine hatch cover or engine box on single-engine models, and on the underside of the starboard engine hatch cover or engine box on twin-engine models.

You may also find it stamped into the aft surface of the forward header of the engine hatch on single-engine models, and stamped into the aft surface of the forward header of the port engine hatch on twin-engine models.

It could also be stamped into the top edge of the engine stringer starboard next to the engine coupling on single-engine models, and stamped into the top edge of the inboard stringer, port engine, next to the engine coupling on twin-engine models.

They are also sometimes found on top of the wood towing bitt, on the aft face of the bow block,

Above: The tell-tale bleached mahogany kingplank of a classic postwar Chris-Craft Runabout. *Classic Boating*

on the extreme forward inboard surface of the port toe rail, or on the aft face of the stem midway between chine and sheer.

On sport boats and runabouts they may be stamped into the forward surface of the aft deck beam if the seat back is removable.

On Corsair Division boats, they may be on the exterior surface of the port bow, just aft of the stem. They may also be stamped into the engine mounting pads on outboards, and into a transom frame or other wood member near the transom. If there is no wood surface available, the number may be glassed into the inboard side of the transom.

On fiberglass cruisers and sailboats, the hull number can be found glassed over on the interior surface of the port hull side, forward of the foremost bulkhead. Outboard sailboat models will have the number stamped into the engine pad.

For more information about the Mariner's Museum or the Chris-Craft Collection, contact them directly at 100 Museum Drive, Newport News, VA 23606-3759; 757-591-7785.

Other Resources

Antique & Classic Boat Society
315-686-4104
The Rudder (newsletter)

Chris-Craft Antique Boat Club
217 South Adams Street
Tallahassee, FL 32301-1708
850-224-BOAT (2628)
www.chris-craft.org

The Brass Bell, quarterly newsletter
President Wilson Wright

Classic Boating magazine
280 Lac La Belle Drive
Oconomowoc, WI 53066-1648
414-567-4800

Classic Speedboats 1916–1939
By Gerald Guetat
Published 1997 by MBI Publishing Company
PO Box 1, 729 Prospect Ave.
Osceola, WI 54020
800-826-6600

Cutwater
By Robert Bruce Duncan
Published 1993 by Top Ten Publishing Corporation
42 Digital Drive, Suite 5
Novato, CA 94949

Gar Wood Boats: Classics of a Golden Era
By Anthony Mollica
Published 1999 by MBI Publishing Company
PO Box 1, 729 Prospect Ave.
Osceola, WI 54020
800-826-6600

The Legend of Chris-Craft, 3rd Ed.
by Jeffrey Rodengen
Published 1998 by Write Stuff Syndicate, Inc.
1515 Southeast 4th Ave.
Fort Lauderdale, FL 33316
305-462-6657

Michigan Maritime Museum
PO Box 534
South Haven, MI 49090
616-637-8078

Real Runabouts Vols. I–VI
By Robert Spelz
Published 1977–1987

Index